HOSPITALITY
— FROM —
WITHIN

By Sarah Dandashy

Copyright © 2021 by Sarah Dandashy

All rights reserved.

Printed in the United States of America

ISBN: 978-0-578-92331-4

Consulting Publisher Live Your Dreams Out Loud Publishing

Cover Photo by: Jorge Orlando Lopez

CONTENTS

DEDICATION AND THANK YOU 7
FOREWORD 9
INTRODUCTION 13
    The Stories Tell It All 15
    Quotes That Inspire 16
    So, Who Am I? 16
CHAPTER 1 – Hospitality From Within 21
    What Does it Mean for Hospitality to Come From Within? 22
    Can Hospitality Be Taught? 23
    At the End of the Day, Why Does it Matter? 26
CHAPTER 2 – The History of Hospitality 29
    A Brief History of the Hospitality Industry 30
    Ancient Hospitality Customs 31
    Evolution of the Hospitality Industry 33
CHAPTER 3 – The Seven Pillars of Hospitality 39
    Service vs. Hospitality 40
    Seven Pillars of Hospitality 41
    Pillar 1: Genuine & Authentic Engagement 42
    Pillar 2: The Art of Listening (and Reading a Guest) 46
    Pillar 3: Make It Personal 48
    Pillar 4: Anticipating Needs 50
    Pillar 5: Consistency 53
    Pillar 6: Efficiency 55
    Pillar 7: Keep It Fresh 56
CHAPTER 4 – The Art of Effective Communication 61

What is Effective Communication 62

Why Communication Matters 64

From Warm Welcomes to Fond Farewells and 66

Delivery Is Everything 67

Proper Language vs Slang 68

Thank You, You're Welcome 69

Match Their Style 69

CHAPTER 5 – The Role of Relationships in Hospitality 73

Hospitality is All About Relationships 74

Internal vs External Hospitality 75

Understanding the Machine 76

An Attitude of Willingness and Awareness 76

The Importance of Interpersonal Abilities 79

Can We Be Friends? The Value of Developing Relationships 79

Helping Guests Foster Their Own Relationships 81

CHAPTER 6 – Culture of Yes, and When to Say No 85

Starting with a "Can-Do" Mindset 86

Yes, and What Is Your Question? 87

No… But Always Have Options 89

Taking Ownership 91

How Ethics Plays into Hospitality 92

How Ethics Plays into Being Genuine & Authentic 93

CHAPTER 7 – Conflict Resolution 97

Conflicts Are Inevitable 98

Steps to Resolving Conflicts & Issues 99

The Art of the Apology 101

Can You Hear Me Now? 103

    Turning Angry Clients Into Life-Long Customers 104

CHAPTER 8 – How to Make the Impossible, Possible **107**

    The Magic Mindset 108

    Pyramid of Service 110

    Finding the Fun: Creativity and Imagination 113

CHAPTER 9 – The Tipping Point: From Four-Star to Five-Star **117**

    Four-Star vs Five-Star Service 118

    The Tipping Point: What Makes Great Service Excellent 118

    Strong Company Culture 121

CHAPTER 10 – Personalized Service in a Digital World **125**

    Understanding Hospitality Technology 126

    The Evolution of Hospitality Tech 126

    Today's Biggest Challenges 130

    High Tech While Remaining High Touch 131

    Use Technology to Do the Heavy Lifting 133

CHAPTER 11 - Conclusion **137**

CHAPTER 12 – Stories from Behind the Desk **143**

    Phone a Friend 145

    Bringing Millie Home 146

    Love Is in the Air 147

    Origami Paper Cranes 148

    Wedding Dress Debacle 149

    25th Wedding Anniversary Celebration 150

    Creating Magical Moments 151

    London - Paris Proposal 152

    My Dear Friend Steven 153

    Misplaced Wallet 154

Excuse Me, I'd Like a Seat for a Teddy Bear… 155

Show of a Lifetime - Grand Ole Opry 156

It Happened During the Day…. 157

Crossing Paths with a Movie Star at 1:00 am 158

The World's Most-Traveled Buttons 159

Needle in a Haystack 160

Christmas on Ice 161

Proposals 'R' Us 163

Personal Connections 164

All They Needed Was a Sign 165

Stars in the Forest 166

Final Thoughts 169

About The Author 171

DEDICATION AND THANK YOU

No book ever written is created alone. Every single page of this book is a result of a team effort. Thank you to everyone who helped along the way.

This book is dedicated to my family, especially to my mother. Thank you for all the experiences you have exposed me to, the opportunities you have encouraged me to take, and for being the most consistent cheerleader and support system in my life. I love you. Also, thank you for your illustration which can be found at the end of the book.

Of course, there are my good friends who have been immensely encouraging and supportive.

Brian Johnson, Sommer Janssen, Sophie Dahan, Kalindra Ashleigh, Anthony Melchiorri, Rupesh Patel, Ellie Goneva, Conor Charles, and Laura Cunningham. Each of you have been amazing throughout this journey. From pep talks to input on rewrites, fonts, content, and more, I appreciate each one of you.

Thank you to my grandparents, the G-units as I like to call them, Lois and Bill, for being such incredible support systems to both myself and the whole family. Especially my late Grandfather who passed just before this book was released. Grandpa, thank you for inspiring all of us to let our work lead the way towards any of our dreams.

And thank you to my dad for checking in and inspiring me to keep going and always find the energy to make any goal a reality.

Then there are always a few monumental moments—seemingly small decisions—that ultimately impact the trajectory of our lives. I have been lucky to have a few of these moments... Thank you to…

Talal Yousif, my cousin, for encouraging me to apply and work at my first hotel, The Four Seasons, Washington DC. He not only introduced me to the world of hotels, but he is even quoted in this book.

Jack Naderkhani, former General Manager of the L'Ermitage, Beverly Hills, for seeing something in me and "gifting" me the opportunity to become a concierge shortly after moving to Los Angeles back in 2005.

James Little, Chef Concierge at The Peninsula Beverly Hills, and my former boss, for being such an inspiration, mentor, and friend, and for helping me so much in fleshing out ideas and concepts for this book.

And a big thank you to The London West Hollywood and all my former co-workers for creating such a supportive environment that allowed me to explore and grow my career.

To all of those who contributed to this book through quotes and stories, thank you. Your hospitality spirit shines through.

Of course, there are many more that I could mention. If you have been a friend or colleague along the way, thank you for being a source of inspiration. You have made more of an impact than you know.

FOREWORD

By Anthony Melchiorri

Elegant. Approachable. Fierce. Delightful.

Those were the words that popped into mind when I first met Sarah. Those are the same words that came to mind as I read Hospitality From Within.

For me, this is the go-to book in the hospitality business.

That might come as a surprise to some people who have heard me often say that hospitality is innate. That hospitality cannot be taught.

After reading this book, I will never say those words again.

Sarah has totally changed my mind. She started in the hospitality business at a very young age. Like many of us, right from the beginning, she found herself in the deep end of the pool. It was sink or swim. As it turned out, I'd call her the Michael Phelps of hospitality. She swam, and she has never stopped.

She is that rare combination of a person who truly listens, who is amazingly self-disciplined, who possesses an incredible work ethic, and has an insatiable desire to serve others.

I loved reading her thoughts on guest recovery, on guest expectations, and on overall guest satisfaction. Sure, those are topics that are brought up in many other books, but what Sarah does in this book - which just can't be found in other books - is to teach that service (not just in hospitality) comes truly from within.

This book is easy to read, but she doesn't leave anything out, making this an important book that really should be part of every business's training.

As she says in the book, "mindset is everything."

And this book has the right mindset.

Human connection is
the cornerstone
of hospitality.

INTRODUCTION

When one thinks of hospitality, immediately what comes to mind are luxury hotels. After all, luxury hotels are the ones who "get it right" when it comes to delivering service. So much more than simply beautiful properties with the finest linens, gorgeous architecture, and exquisite cuisine, luxury hotels always deliver exceptional service. It is this exceptional service—*how* they make you *feel*—that is hospitality.

Hospitality is the warmth, the special moments, and ultimately, the genuine, human connection that makes a service an experience. The beauty of it is that hospitality doesn't need to just exist in hotels or restaurants—hospitality can be embraced and delivered in every customer service business. From the medical industry to financial services, if you have a customer, you have a chance to shower them in hospitality. Treating the customer like a guest is a solid way to turn them into a customer for life, which is a pretty, solid return on investment.

The purpose of this book is to share some insights into hospitality, with a fresh perspective. In a time when the workforce is heavily shifting to encompass more Generation Y and Z employees, technology is challenging traditional norms of service, and the hospitality industry as a whole has been forced to reimagine itself in the midst of a global pandemic. Now more than ever is a time for us to get back in touch with the human aspect of service.

This isn't just a book for those working in a hotel or restaurant. Every business has a customer service component. Some are more obvious or more in-depth than others, but every business has the ability to raise its service standards. By focusing on the customer *experience* and treating their customers as guests, a company can ultimately increase its business. At the end of the day, if a customer leaves *feeling* good, they will continue to support the business, even if the product is mediocre.

The Stories Tell It All

With all this talk about hospitality, it would be remiss of me to lay out a hospitality book without real stories from the frontlines of the industry. True to the service industry, everything we do relies on working with others. There are stories peppered throughout the book. Some stories will correspond with certain chapters to bring to life and to elaborate on the lesson or topic being discussed.

It's often been said that the hotel concierge is the heartbeat of the hotel; this is meaningful on multiple levels. I will be sharing not only a few of my stories but those experiences from some of the best in the industry who I am honored to call colleagues and friends. I hope you enjoy the series of stories from some of the finest Les Clefs d'Or Concierge around the world, illustrating the extent to which hospitality comes from within. It is inspired by passion and a love of creating delightful experiences. There is no better way to illustrate these magical moments than from stories of the ones who do it on a regular basis.

Of course, in true hospitality fashion, all names and identifying details will be changed out of discretion and to protect the privacy of the individuals involved. Looking for a tell-all book? This isn't it.

Quotes That Inspire

As the purpose of this book is to not only educate but also to inspire, I have selected a few powerful and motivating quotes from thought leaders within the industry who have inspired *me*. After all, hospitality is a continual journey—one where we are constantly learning from our guests, each other, and those who have gone before us. I am and will continue to be a firm believer that we all rise together. I truly hope you are left inspired by this book to not only elevate your standards but to inspire those with whom you work. As an industry that relies so much on teamwork, I want to pass on these lessons to encourage new generations in the industry and workforce.

So, Who Am I?

I am a hospitality professional with nearly 20 years of guest-facing, luxury hotel experience. I was lucky enough to fall into the industry by chance. Introduced to the world of luxury hotels by my cousin, he implored me to get a job at the Four Seasons, Washington DC, while I was attending Georgetown University. I will forever be grateful for that opportunity and training. When it comes to hotels, there are two ways in which you can train for the industry. The first is by attending a prestigious hospitality school, such as Les Roches, Ecole Hôtelière de Lausanne, Cornell University, or UNLV. Secondly, you can get immediate hands-on experience from a five-star hotel company with an excellent training program, such as Four Seasons or Ritz Carlton. I, by chance, ended up with the latter.

Fast forward a few years, and I found myself in Los Angeles. I enjoyed my experience of working in hotels while attending college, so I figured landing a job in a hotel would be a great way to get settled into a new city. I had hoped the job would provide an immediate network of friends, a chance to meet interesting locals, and connect with individuals who passed through town. Another pivotal moment happened when the then general manager of the L'Ermitage, Beverly Hills, offered me a concierge position. I had no lobby or front desk experience, and most of my background had been in F&B. But clearly, as he could tell, I had the right attributes. Thus began my concierge journey.

Of those years spent on the hospitality frontlines, 15 years were as a concierge. Seven of those years were as a Les Clefs d'Or Concierge, the same organization that graciously awarded me with an international award equivalent to "Best Young Concierge." For those who might not be familiar, Les Clefs d'Or is the international professional organization of hotel concierges. Becoming a member is a feat in and of itself. But once invited, you are immediately welcomed into an incredible community of some of the best of the best around the world. For those who have ever watched the famous movie by Wes Anderson, *The Grand Budapest Hotel,* you will appreciate the camaraderie, connection, and support of the community on a global level. Becoming a Les Clefs d'Or concierge truly elevated not only my standards but myself as a professional.

Titles and organizations aside, it was my day-to-day guest interactions as well as the strong community of like-minded colleagues and incredible mentors that truly shaped my experience. The hospitality industry is best learned in action, on the fly, and with a strong team. No day is ever the same, no request ever identical, and no experience ever replicable. Hospitality schools provide the building blocks and tools, helping to shape the mindset, but it is in the practice where the *art of hospitality* is finessed and fine-tuned.

A few years back, I created the online brand, Ask A Concierge®. Combining my love for travel, hospitality, and life, I have produced over 300 videos covering everything from destinations to travel tips to interviews with colleagues. Another "happy accident," as I like to call it, was that creating Ask A Concierge® gave my career a new life and reinvigorated my passion for my profession. Going beyond my traditional concierge desk to a virtual one, I found a new appreciation in guiding my daily guests as well as reaching and inspiring travelers around the world. Not to mention, it also opened me up to a whole new world of possibilities and opportunities.

Thank you for picking up this book. I hope you learn a thing or two, solidify ideas you already had, or better yet, become inspired to look at hospitality in a new light.

> True hospitality is this genuine willingness to tend to others. To put others' needs before yours, even if just for a moment. To entertain, to delight, to surprise—all motivated by finding purpose in creating joy for others.

CHAPTER 1

Hospitality From Within

What Does it Mean for Hospitality to Come From Within?

The notion that *hospitality comes from within* encompasses a few meanings. Of course, initially, it reflects that hospitality comes from a genuine desire to help, please, or provide service. More than that, it is intuitive, where service is somewhat instinctive. To a certain degree, it is and can be, but it must also be taught and finessed through education, training, and personal experience.

We have often heard the phrase "hospitality from the heart," which also taps into the notion that hospitality comes from within. This sense of caring, and possibly even loving, is what drives hospitality from the heart.

On a broader scale, understanding hospitality in terms of a business, hospitality starts from the internal culture. As many great hospitality leaders have shared, from Danny Meyer to Sir Richard Branson, hospitality starts with your employees. If your employees are treated well, they in turn will provide exceptional service to your guests.

This leads us to the next point of discussion: can hospitality be taught?

Can Hospitality Be Taught?

It has been said over and over that true hospitality cannot be taught. One must hire for personality, as skills are teachable. To a degree, this is true. It is always better to hire someone with the right attitude.

>
> You can teach the spirit and service to people who have an innate desire to serve.
>
> HOLLY STIEL
> THANK YOU VERY MUCH INC

So, what makes for the right attitude? It is a combination of the following:

Naturally Kind & Empathetic

This is more than being emotionally intelligent. Emotional intelligence is often understood as the ability to recognize and manage your emotions and the emotions of others, as well as the ability to handle interpersonal relationships judiciously and empathetically. In other words, seek to hire those with warmth and the capacity to understand others.

Adaptability

Regardless of role or job position, the ability to adapt to change is critical in hospitality. How often have we heard people say, "No day is the same," in their hospitality career? A lot. From shift work to being a guest-driven business, true hospitality professionals must be adaptable—and it is even better when they have a positive attitude about it

Mindfulness

The ability to understand one's role in the bigger picture, and the impact of follow-through in tasks, makes mindfulness a critical trait. This level of conscientiousness reflects the ability to think beyond oneself, taking ownership or responsibility for one's actions. Mindfulness is incredibly important in hospitality.

Willingness to Learn

This is a step beyond adaptability because change is inevitable. A willingness to learn is part of a "growth mindset," where one is open to identifying their weaknesses and then actively working on improving them. One must have the mindset that learning will always positively benefit oneself and that one has the capability to improve.

Team Player Attitude

The reality is the hospitality industry is like a giant machine where everyone plays a part. Embracing the spirit of teamwork is essential to a career in hospitality. Even though this is something that we, as humans, have been taught since a young age, the fact of the matter is, some play well with others better than others.

Optimistic

What ultimately weaves all these traits together is a positive attitude. It may sound cliche but believing that there's a positive outcome in any and all challenging situations will help one navigate the day-to-day of a job in hospitality. The upside is that it will also inspire other people to *really* want to work with that person.

> If you look after your staff, they will look after your customer. It's that simple.
>
> SIR RICHARD BRANSON

These traits are often described as soft skills. Regardless of job position, these characteristics can make for great employees. In the hospitality industry, be it hotels or restaurants, it is the service, AKA the employees, that can make a good establishment great. The business can have all the physical components of a five-star establishment, from marble floors to high thread counts and the finest cuisine, but the service levels must match or exceed the tangible offerings or the guest experience will suffer.

After all, hospitality is the art of caring. It is more than an untamed natural emotion. In the world of hospitality, caring can be a craft - expertly executed and fine-tuned to go beyond cultural and even language barriers.

I will even take it a step further and argue that hospitality can be taught. Simply put, the best way to teach hospitality is to lead by example. Doing unto others, then pointing out what was done and how it made them feel, is the best way to inspire the spirit of hospitality. With the right guidance, I believe the essence and core traits of hospitality can be taught.

> While one may argue you are born with such soft skills, I am also convinced that such traits can be taught and further developed under the right corporate culture and mindset.
>
> TALAL YOUSIF
> EXECUTIVE HOSPITALITY ADVISOR

At the End of the Day, Why Does it Matter?

In a world where technology is permeating more and more of our day-to-day, hospitality brings the human element back into our lives. Sometimes we don't even realize we miss it until we experience it again.

The pandemic of 2020 taught us that we, as humans, crave connectivity. Humans are naturally social animals. Of course, some are more social than others, but in general, humans want to interact and belong with other humans. Hospitality would not exist without the human element.

People are the key component of hospitality. Not robots, not AI-generated texts. Those might be helpful tools to efficiently get tasks done or to assist in delivering a service, but service and hospitality are very different. Service is the nuts and bolts of handling a task or providing information to a guest. Hospitality is the interaction; it is how one makes a guest feel. Hospitality is the *experience* of the service.

"I can teach anybody to be a concierge. I can't teach someone to be nice, to be empathetic, to be caring, you know, but I can help them learn how to be that way by leading by example and putting them in an environment where they do that every day. And they see the benefits of it. Not just for the person they're helping, but also for themselves. You can provide the environment and the examples where you hope they'll learn it."

JAMES G. LITTLE
CHEF CONCIERGE PENINSULA
BEVERLY HILLS

> Hospitality, as a concept, is innate to us as human beings. Of course, it can be further emphasized by nurture and by the culture you live in, but this idea of being open to host and to welcome people comes naturally to us.

BASHAR WALI
CEO OF THIS ASSEMBLY

CHAPTER 2

The History of Hospitality

A Brief History of the Hospitality Industry

In order to better understand and define where society may be going in the near future with hospitality, one must first take a moment to understand the history of the hospitality industry.

First, let's recognize the origin of the word *hospitality*. It is derived from the French word *hospice* which means "house of assistance" or "shelter for travelers and pilgrims." Although the original word is still very much used today in a different context, at its core, it is still about helping, taking care, and evening pampering others.

As an industry, hospitality has evolved to incorporate a large range of fields within the service sector, from hotels to restaurants to transportation to even spas. It is no longer reserved for those traveling just for business, as it once was centuries ago. With the rise of disposable income and increased availability of leisure time, the hospitality industry has become the focus of where individuals choose to spend their time off. Even more so today, where there is an increased emphasis on "experiences," the hospitality industry must rely even more on its service core.

>
> We were born to serve and our sense of hospitality is deeply rooted in empathy, emotional intelligence, altruism, and genuine care.
>
> TALAL YOUSIF
> EXECUTIVE HOSPITALITY ADVISOR

Many of the components that define "service" are in fact customs that have been around since the beginning of time. As much as it is human nature to be hospitable to strangers, it was also reinforced in many ancient societies as a moral institution. These customs and traditions can even be traced back to Biblical writings and concepts.

Ancient Hospitality Customs

Of course, centuries ago, travel was a far more rigorous and exhausting feat. Due to this, travelers were reliant on the hospitality of strangers. Travelers were revered and celebrated, and hosting a guest was considered admirable. This is an interesting point and emphasizes how full circle we have come with the rise and popularity of Airbnb, which will be discussed later. But more than just welcoming travelers, there were other customs that became prevalent in various cultures that we still see to this day.

The Ancient Greeks saw hospitality as a commandment and requirement from the gods. They actually believed that turning away visitors would result in punishment. As a result, the Ancient Greeks strived to be the best of hosts, reveling in their hospitable reputation. After all, being a good host was a sign of wealth. Thus, from Ancient Greeks, the notice of excellent service became equated with hospitality, which still rings true to this day.

The Ancient Romans focused on a different way of welcoming guests and travelers: through food. By celebrating guests with feasts and exchanging gifts or tokens, visitors were greeted with a welcome kiss and often wined and dined. As the trade networks expanded throughout the Roman Empire, Romans would strive to impress their guests with extravagant fare, beautiful tableware, and various forms of entertainment. This over-the-top extravaganza reflected the host's wealth, status, and sophistication to his guests, oftentimes with the intention of outdoing his elite friends and colleagues.

Ancient Chinese and other Asian cultures also placed high importance on hospitality. From foot washing to offering tea, they seemed to treat travelers and guests as gods. The Ancient Chinese in particular would always welcome their guests by offering their best teas. Influencing the tea culture that is still alive to this day, this directly paved the way for the popular tradition of offering a welcome drink in many of today's hotels.

Throughout time, across the globe, and regardless of local cultures, the belief of being an exemplary host was a common theme. From offering exceptional service to providing lavish feasts to greeting guests with welcome beverages, the reputation of being a generous host was highly desired. Each of these ancient customs, though different in detail, have shaped the hospitality industry as we know it. The human connection of customer service is the cornerstone of the hospitality industry, not just in the past, but in the present and certainly into the future.

Evolution of the Hospitality Industry: From Ancient Greece to the Modern Hospitality Industry

The concept of facilities offering hospitality services dates as far back as the Greek and Roman antiquities. Beginning with the Greeks who offered thermal baths as a place for rest and relaxation in local villages, it was not long after that the Romans built large villas to house travelers who were on the road conducting government business. The Romans then expanded into Europe and the Middle East establishing thermal baths. These thermal baths were the precursor to the modern-day spa, and the large villas were the foundation for today's hotel industry.

The Medieval Period saw a rise in merchant travelers from England to the Middle East along popular trade routes, also famously known as the Silk Road. Throughout Europe, an increasing number of private residences and alehouses were turned into inns. Inns became available at intervals of 20 to 25 miles, which was equivalent to a day's worth of travel. Innkeepers were generally wealthy and part of the urban elite. They took part in local government and acted as expediters and banking agents. They also served as local hubs in the late medieval system of commerce.

Many travelers of nobility found respite in monasteries. And in the Middle East, caravanserais, inns with central courtyards, became prevalent with the caravan culture dominating the area.

Marco Polo is highly referenced during this period, as he was the first, and the most well-known, merchant to leave a detailed chronicle of his travels in his book, *The Travels of Marco Polo,* c. 1300. His work influenced many famous travelers to come, the most notable being Christopher Columbus, as well as literature and the creation of the Fra Mauro map.

The Fra Mauro map was significant as it represented the first time that a scientific approach influenced the way a map was made versus the maps in the past. Previously, maps had been created from geography described in the Bible. With the Fra Mauro map, scientific accuracy finally had sway over religious and traditional beliefs.

After the Middle Ages, we can look to the French Revolution as another period where there was a drastic change in hospitality and hotels. This was the era where gastronomy was born, and hotels became more than places to rest and sleep. Hotels began to grow in grandeur and cater to wealthier clients, and the modern-day restaurant was born. Chefs dominated the scene in France and slowly began to increase in influence. Although a gradual growth, it was not until the early 19th century that hotels of such opulence really gained popularity.

The modern hospitality industry really grew in the 19th and 20th centuries to meet societal demands. Luxury hotels, landmarks like The Savoy in London and the Ritz in Paris, established a new level of standards and expectations in hospitality. As countries around the world grew and developed as industrial nations, hotels reflected this prosperity and catered to the increasing number of travelers.

Hospitality trends went from opulent in the early 1900s, with floral designs and brass beds, to a more scaled-back design in the 1920s, when the trend was "less is more." As more people had increased leisure time and paid vacation from work, hotels continued to increase in demand.

The first motel, or 'motor hotel,' catering to those traveling by automobile, opened in 1925, the Motel Inn in San Luis Obispo, California. A combination of offering an inexpensive overnight option for travelers and the completion of Route 66, motels grew in popularity in the 1920s. Of course, this all changed drastically in 1929 with the start of The Great Depression in the United States. Despite the dip in growth during the 1930s, the hospitality industry really expanded in the 1940s and 1950s. After the Second World War, the 1940s saw a boom in the economy and an increase in leisure travel and vacation time. Casinos grew in popularity during this time. They became attractive destinations, luring travelers with the excitement of gambling and lower room rates.

In the 1950s, more people owned their own cars, allowing individuals and families to travel more for business and leisure. It was during this period, the 1950s and 1960s, that the hospitality industry developed more structure. With an increasing number of people traveling, all the various economic backgrounds, and for differing reasons from leisure to business, hotels shifted their focus to property and in-room amenities. From ice and vending machines on hotel floors to the introduction of 24-hour room service, hotel chains focused on setting themselves apart from the rest.

The latter part of the 20th century saw a rise in hotel chains and established brands. With larger pools of resources, hotels were able to tackle hospitality and travel trends, pushing to evolve and innovate significantly. Customer service and amenities have been the driving force in what gives these brands a competitive edge. Today, the hospitality industry encompasses many niche markets, from apartment rentals to resorts to boutique hotels to economy and luxury hotels. The landscape of hospitality is highly compartmentalized, yet technology is an ever-present component.

Modern hospitality cannot be viewed without acknowledging its relationship with technology, which we will discuss in a later chapter. Economic and social developments in the 19th and 20th centuries inspired massive changes in the hotel industry, but technology, becoming so much more intertwined with everyday life, has had an exponential influence. Traveling truly was no longer solely for the privileged upper classes. The invention of trains, automobiles, and planes as well as increased vacations and reduced working hours made it possible for the average person to indulge in travel.

KEY DATES IN THE
HISTORY OF HOSPITALITY

707 AD
Nisiyama Onsen Keiunkan, Yamanashi
The world's oldest hotel. It's been run by 52 generations of the same family.

1282
Florence, Italy
The first innkeepers association was formed. Their goal was to turn hospitality into a business. Inns became licensed and were permitted to import and resell wine. By the year 1290, 86 inns in Florence were members of the guild.

1794
The City Hotel, New York
The first building in America that was specifically built to be a hotel. Because it also offered meeting rooms, it became a prime social destination shortly after opening its doors.

1797
The Lismore House Hotel
The first hotel built in Ireland.

1805
The York Hotel, Toronto, Canada
Canada's first hotel.

1876
Mandarin Oriental, Siam 1880 (Bangkok)
The official opening year of the Oriental Hotel, the origin of the Oriental side of the Mandarin Oriental.

1887
Raffles Hotel, Singapore
Offering 10 rooms in an old bungalow-style building overlooking the beach and the South China Sea.

1900
Prinzessin Victoria Luise
First cruise ship built and sailed.

1925
The Motel Inn
Located in San Luis Obispo, California, it was the first motel in the world.

1928
Peninsula, Hong Kong
It was billed as the "finest hotel east of the Suez" and went on to be known as the Grand Dame.

1929
The Royal York, Toronto, Canada
Its kitchen was Canada's largest hotel kitchen when the Royal York first opened, capable of producing over 15,000 French bread rolls a day.

1950S
Mayfair Hotel in downtown St. Louis
Actor Cary Grant requested chocolates on his pillows while staying at the luxurious Mayfair Hotel, thus starting the trend of chocolates on pillows at turndown.

2015
First World Hotel, Malaysia
World's Largest hotel has 7,351 rooms and suites.

2018
Ahmed Abdul Rahim Al Attar Tower, Genvora Hotel, Dubai
Tallest hotel in the world.

> Service is transactional, while hospitality is experiential.

CHAPTER 3

The Seven Pillars of Hospitality

Service vs. Hospitality

In order to best analyze the success of a business, it is necessary not only to identify the customer or guest touch points, but also to recognize the quality of services delivered. Ultimately, the higher the quality of service, the higher the chances are of business success overall. So how do we measure service quality? First, we must understand the difference between service and hospitality.

In very broad strokes, service is the mere act of doing something or providing a simple task for someone. Businesses are built around offering services. Providing a service isn't necessarily fancy. In fact, service is truly, at its core, transactional. It is A + B = C. Where hospitality comes into play is the *experience* of delivering and receiving that service.

>
> Service is what you deliver, but hospitality is how you make people feel.
> BASHAR WALI
> CEO OF THIS ASSEMBLY

Hospitality is the art of delivering a service. There are so many nuances, colors, and flavors to it that make it specific to not only providers, but to the business, and on an even larger scale, to the brand. Hospitality is experiential. People not only spend more money on experiences than simple transactions but the more money they spend on an experience, the higher their expectations.

In the world of hotels, guests are not only expecting more luxurious accommodations, but also for the service experience to be at a higher level. This is not only hospitality, but it is also how a hotel is valued.

> 66
> If one views the hotel as the hardware, the staff are definitely the software. And both coalesce together to create an emotional guest experience —one that inspires visitors to return time and time again.
>
> SERGE ETHUIN
> GENERAL MANAGER OF THE
> HOTEL METROPOLE MONTE CARLO

Seven Pillars of Hospitality

Considering that hospitality is arguably an art form, it begs the question: How can hospitality be dissected? What are the key components of hospitality?

Interestingly enough, hospitality is the art of making someone feel a certain way—welcomed, understood, and cared for. One can argue that there are infinite combinations of actions that can influence a guest's experience. Boiled down, I've discovered that there are really seven main pillars of hospitality. And like any good recipe, you might add a little more of this or that to make your hospitality experience different and unique to you.

The seven pillars of hospitality are:

1. Genuine & Authentic Engagement
2. The Art of Listening (and Reading a Guest)
3. Making It Personal
4. Anticipating Needs
5. Consistency
6. Efficiency
7. Keeping It Fresh

Pillar 1: Genuine & Authentic Engagement

In today's world, we have the smartest consumers we have ever had in history. Customers have access to the most information than they have ever had, and therefore, they are truly adept at knowing what they want and sifting through the inauthentic in favor of more authentic interactions.

What do we mean by being authentic and genuine? These words often seem interchangeable. *Authentic* refers to how you are being yourself. This is how you really are inside — how you think, feel, believe, and the like. *Genuine* is all about how you relate to other people. Consumers and guests in today's world are seeking interactions that are not only genuine but delivered by someone authentically.

The #1 Rule for Engagement:
Be interested… genuinely.

Of course, we can break down the specifics of how we should interact with guests in technical terms. The following are best practices for how to set the stage to engage with a guest in person.

Eye Contact

Eye contact is one of the first ways to interact with a guest. Eye contact allows you to acknowledge a guest before even speaking with them. As you may have noticed, it is also the first part of the 10-5-3 Rule. It all begins with eye contact, then a nod or verbal greeting can follow.

Smile

If eyes are the window to the soul, then smiles are the front door. A smile says a thousand words. Smiles are contagious, and they are one of the most important physical visual cues in the world of hospitality.

Be Present

In the service industry, we are always multitasking, managing several requests at one time. Therefore, it is imperative that one stays present. Being present allows you to pick up on nuances and details that a guest might be sharing. It also is one of the most important aspects of being genuinely engaged.

And then there is the 10-5-3 Rule:

At 10 feet, look up from what you are doing and acknowledge the customer with direct eye contact and a nod.

At 5 feet, smile. Not just with your mouth, but with your eyes as well.

At 3 feet, verbally greet the guest with a specific time-of-day greeting ("Good morning"). Keep in mind to use a tone of voice appropriate to the location or area where you interact with the guest.

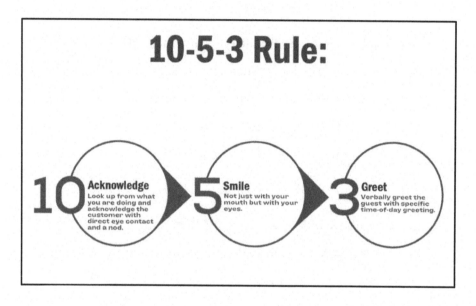

Life in hospitality would be so simple if this was the only means of interacting with a guest. But the challenge doesn't end there, because, in any guest/customer-facing position, we are continuously balancing guest interactions not only in person but also on the phone and digitally.

Personal interactions rely on physical and audible cues as well as language. Each of these working together paints an experience. Once you eliminate any one of these components, the others become that much more crucial to delivering the right message or experience. For example, phone interactions take out the visual, but you still have the audible as well as language to utilize as tools. This means your tone of voice is extremely important. They say that you can hear a smile on the phone, and it's true. Smiling while on the phone will certainly influence the tone in which you speak, and of course, word choice and language is even more important.

Now living in the digital world that we are in today, texts and emails are another important way in which we communicate. The challenge is we now lose both the physical and the audible elements of communication, and thereby can only rely on language. This is where word choice, positive phrases, and appropriate use of punctuation are invaluable. And don't rely on emojis. We aren't there just yet.

> In the end, recognition is about serving those we want to celebrate. And service is not about the giver; it is about the recipient.
>
> DR. BRYAN WILLIAMS
> KEYNOTE SPEAKER &
> AUTHOR

Ultimately, given all these technical aspects of engagement and communication, you want to be yourself. As we discussed at the beginning, you want to be authentic. After all, guests respond favorably to authenticity. In the world of hospitality, it is the human element that we connect with. Being authentic is the best way to establish these connections, and ultimately, to form relationships.

Relationships are a series of interactions. This level of engagement is far richer and more valuable than the transaction of service. Relationships create long-lasting and repeat customers, which is something that every business strives for.

Pillar 2: The Art of Listening (and Reading a Guest)

The concept of listening seems very simple, and it is. The reality is that many people don't listen as much as they should. Understandably so, as every moment we have countless thoughts racing through our heads. But when we truly focus and take in what the other person is saying, that is where a true connection can begin to grow.

In the world of hospitality, it is extremely important to listen to guests. Guests share many clues in what they say, in the stories they share, and in the quips they make. If we truly tune in, we can learn so much about the other person. We must also listen to *how* something is being said, by reading body language and picking up on what is *not* being said.

Being non-judgmental is another key component of listening. If we are too quick to judge, our thoughts are immediately elsewhere, taking us away from the conversation or exchange at hand. Of course, it can be tricky to not make swift judgments. We are human, after all, and so much of our outlook or our lens is colored by past experiences. This is not to say that you should avoid making judgments altogether. That would be both impossible and foolish. While deductive reasoning relies on judgments, it is completely necessary once given enough information on which to act.

The point is to not make judgments while engaged with a guest or person so that you can focus on listening and absorbing as much information in the moment as possible.

Being a strong listener also means that you ask questions. And there is such a beautiful relationship and outcome to asking questions. Asking questions does two things. One, it leads to more information about a person. And two, it makes the other person feel important. (Assuming the question doesn't feel like an interrogation, but an easy inquiry based in curiosity and interest, so there isn't judgment in the question.) People love to talk about themselves. This isn't a bad thing; it is simply human nature.

When people talk about themselves, they feel like they are the center of attention. Now translating this to the world of hospitality, this is when people remark that they feel hospitality the most. They truly feel cared for, accepted, and ultimately connected. Humans crave connection just as much as they crave comfort and familiarity. This is why hospitality is so important to businesses: the feeling of hospitality will lead guests, clients, customers, and coworkers to return again and again.

Arguably more important is what you do with the information you have learned from speaking with a guest or colleague. The most expected response is part of active listening, where you ask questions, nod, and provide physical clues that you are invested in the interaction. The five-star, next-level, reply is taking the initiative to do something thoughtful for the guest or colleague based on what they shared. This demonstrates that you were listening and that you thought of them afterwards, and they were inspired to act upon a part of the conversation. Thoughtfulness is where true hospitality come to life.

> " It's the people, the staff, that brings beautiful hotels to life.
>
> ROBERT MARKS
> CHEF CONCIERGE AND PAST
> PRESIDENT OF LES CLEFS D'OR
> USA

Pillar 3: Make It Personal

In hospitality, there is no such thing as "one size fits all." Every interaction should be personalized, nothing should be generic. As we discussed before, today's guests and customers are too knowledgeable and too astute to be impressed by generalities. In fact, they commonly have high expectations and have usually have "seen it all." To push beyond the expected and truly impress today's consumers/guests, we have to make it personal.

Not only should the interactions and services be personalized, but the service provider or employee should be unique. As we discussed in breaking down the difference between authentic and genuine, people respond to genuine. As an employer, you should absolutely encourage your employees to be themselves when they engage with guests.

It's all about the *personality* in personalization.

We are seeing a shift in what travelers want. Guests don't want overly scripted, and it comes across false and ingenuine. As a result, big hospitality brands with very distinct standards are veering away from requiring specifically scripted interactions. Even Forbes Travel Guide, who is responsible for awarding hotels with their coveted star rating, continues to evolve their service standards. For example, instead of always sending a written confirmation printed on letterhead to a guest's room, it is acceptable to notify guests in other ways, such as texting. Even as things change, the luxury guest experience must remain positive, meaningful, and personal. In doing so, properties will continue to win guest loyalty and build confidence. Trust is a key component of personalized service.

Personalized service doesn't mean that there are *no standards*. It simply means the standards are customizable. There must always be parameters in which an employee or agent can play while still maintaining brand standards. You may want unscripted interactions, but there still needs to be minimum requirements to ensure a consistent execution of expectations are met. After all, brand standards play a significant role in appealing to guests. They come to learn what to expect and oftentimes make their decisions based on those expectations.

LESSON:

Don't just make the guest feel good.

Make them feel important.

While we should strive to provide unique and personalized interactions, keep in mind the brand that you are representing. Every interaction matters.

Personalized interactions don't just make a guest feel good; they should make them feel important. One might think making a guest feel good and making them feel important go hand in hand, but there are slight nuances that differentiate the two. We make a guest feel good by welcoming them and by actively listening. To make a guest feel important, you have to go above and beyond and offer extra, unexpected services. The goal should be to inspire a guest to say, "Wow, that was so thoughtful." That is when memorable experiences are created.

>
> I love creating experiences that elevate humans, that makes them feel respected, cared for, deeply rested, fed, nourished, and refreshed.
>
> BASHAR WALI
> CEO OF THIS ASSEMBLY

Pillar 4: Anticipating Needs

For those not new to the world of hospitality, the concept of *anticipating needs* is not new. In fact, anticipating needs has been so ingrained into our psyche that we begin to think of the next steps the moment we put on our nametags. But even though we all can talk ad nauseam about anticipating needs, it is still important to break down *how* and *why* we strive to anticipate needs.

The concept of anticipating needs means that you have an idea of the next steps that will need to be executed and can immediately offer solutions prior to being asked. Following the footsteps of genuine engagement, if you are truly engaged as a hospitality professional, you have an idea of potential next requests. It includes anticipating what a customer might have *wanted* to ask for but "didn't want to be a bother," what they didn't know enough to ask for, and what they haven't gotten around yet to ask for—in other words, their *unexpressed* needs and wishes.

> *For example:*
>
> A guest calls down and requests a car service to be booked to go to the airport in the morning. After obtaining all the necessary details to book the car service, the agent can offer to arrange for a wake-up call and even put in an order with room service. By doing so, the agent is acknowledging a few extra steps that the guest will likely go through in the morning and offering solutions to make the morning that much easier.

Anticipating needs is more than being 'nice'; it is about delivering 'thoughtful service.'

Another aspect of anticipating needs is also anticipating the next questions. If a guest places a request that you need to find more information on, don't just find answers to the specific questions you were asked. Put yourself in the guest's shoes and ask what could be the next question they might ask you. This in turn avoids going back and forth with a guest. Anticipate the questions they might ask so you have all the answers when you return to the guest with information the first time. Two wins happen from this. One, you minimize the time spent on that request and get to the answer or next steps more efficiently. And two, you again demonstrate that the guest is important by valuing their request. You will also establish credibility and trust with your guests, earning their confidence that you will look after them and make their stay seamless.

Ultimately, *anticipating needs* is about the 'thoughtful' element. By offering a unique suggestion that a guest hadn't thought of or creating a special surprise inspired by a comment said in passing, these moments serve as the tipping point for excellent service. There is no better way to show genuine engagement than by offering a

>
> Sometimes the million-dollar car is less meaningful than the smile and spark in the eyes of a surprised lady at the (not forgotten) anniversary.
>
> SASCHA DOMM
> CHEF CONCIERGE
> BRENNERS PARK-HOTEL & SPA, BADEN-BADEN

thoughtful touch or suggestion that shows you are thinking not only ahead of the guest but in their best interest.

Pillar 5: Consistency

If we break it down to understand that the product that we are selling is service, then consistency in how we deliver that service is imperative. We wouldn't buy a specific product at the grocery store if we didn't know the quality would be the same every time. Brands are built on the consistency of the product that they sell, and in the case of the hospitality industry, we sell a specific level of service.

LESSON:

The mark of a true professional is *consistently* delivering great service, regardless of guest, circumstance, or even personal distractions.

The tricky part of consistency is that our product is based on people. People deliver the service. Whenever people are involved, one must always allow for a margin of error. This is why consistency is extremely important in the world of hospitality. The how and the level at which we deliver service must be consistent for every single interaction, regardless of who is providing the service and to whom they are providing the service.

Consistency can be looked at on the macro-level (think brand standards) and on the micro-level (think personal standards). But to be successful, both the macro and the micro must be aligned. For example, say we choose to stay at a Four Seasons hotel, now if we have previously experienced a Four Seasons property before, we have an idea of what to expect. The brand standards that the Four Seasons have established a sense of what we can expect, and it is the consistency in those standards across destinations, countries, and cultures that makes it a brand. The entire Four Seasons experience is what is being sold.

> **❝**
> I think consistency and style are important. The number one thing is how you treat your people. People flourish in an environment where they know the leader has a certain amount of stability and treats them well. They know what to expect day in and day out, and then you lay out the expectations. What I've always been told, which is very true, is to be consistent with your people, even when you're not feeling it, because however you go is how the rest of your team goes.
>
> RAUL LEAL
> FORMER CEO OF VIRGIN HOTEL GROUP

Similarly, on the micro-level, personal standards of engagement are equally as important to the entire experience. This means that no matter who a guest engages with, be it an operator, pool attendant, housekeeper, engineer, or front desk agent, the guest will be greeted with the same level of service. Of course, the interactions may be different due to their respective roles, but it is *how* they deliver their service (and the heart behind it) that must remain consistent.

Since hospitality is inherently intangible, the consistency at which it is delivered is exceptionally important. Consistency tells a story. But more than that, consistency sets expectations, it builds trust, and ultimately, it creates value.

Pillar 6: Efficiency

Efficiency is another critical pillar of hospitality. It is more than how one provides a service, but it is also how quickly it takes to deliver that service. One could go above and beyond and have an incredible guest interaction, but if the task is done too late, it is a moot point. A good job done late is ineffective. Similarly, time is the one thing everyone wants more of, and it can't be replaced. Efficiency feeds into "the luxury of time," which is a critical part of any service, and especially true to delivering five-star service.

An example of this can easily be seen in restaurants. A guest could place a very specific order, and the chef could put together the most thoughtful plate. But if the server delays bringing out the food, it will be cold and defeat the purpose of all the great work done by the chef. Similarly, in a hotel, a guest might need to have a beautiful flower arrangement delivered to a business before the end of the day. Even if the most beautiful flower arrangement was set up with some of the rarest flowers, if it is delivered too late, it is simply too late.

In a time when technology is literally at our fingertips and in the palms of our hands, efficiency must always be part of the hospitality equation. Timeliness equals importance. A timely response tells the guest that their request matters, which in turn, tells the guest that they matter.

Done is not better than perfect. Done correctly is.

And done too late is simply not good enough.

Your guest is at the center of their universe, so it is imperative that you make them feel like the center of yours as well. How do we do this? We determine what matters to them and make it seem like it matters to us. I say "make it seem" that way because we are running a business. We are juggling so many guests and jobs, it would actually be impossible to solely focus on one guest. Then again, this is all about the *magic of hospitality*. It is the illusion that we create or the show that happens on stage. From a guest's perspective, they don't need to see everything that happens behind the scenes. They too have bought into the illusion and want to be surprised with the end result.

Pillar 7: Keep It Fresh

Once one has mastered all the other pillars of hospitality, it is equally as important to remember to keep it fresh—not only to ourselves as hospitality professionals but also to the guests. Regardless of how many interactions you have, you have to keep your attitude fresh. Believe me, I understand how mundane it can feel to repeatedly tell a new guest the directions to the restaurant. "Down the hall and on the left." But you always have to put yourself in their shoes. If it is a guest's first time coming to a property or business, and they truly do not know, a salty attitude is a horrible impression to give them.

Rule:

The best way to keep it fresh is to see it

Through their eyes.

There have been many times where I felt as though my patience was being tested. I, as we all are, am human. It would be in those moments where I didn't want to give it my all that I would think about it from their perspective. Imagine, what if this family had saved up all year just to go on this truly special vacation only to be greeted by an annoyed front desk agent? Or what if the nervous guest was coming in to treat his girlfriend to a special dinner and propose later that evening only to have someone sigh at a request for a certain type of wine.

> **"**
> One of the ways to keep it fresh is to actually pay attention to the people you're serving. Remember, it is fresh for them. And, it's new for you because they're a different person than your last interaction.
> ―――――
> HOLLY STIEL
> THANK YOU VERY MUCH INC

When you think about the guest's experience through their lens and treat every experience as though it might be a significant moment for the guest, it shifts your attitude. I know I certainly would not want to be the sore spot on what would have been a special occasion or a once-in-a-lifetime moment for someone. This might seem extreme, but these are all very real situations and events that we are, by chance, a part of. Always keep your attitude fresh.

Every guest or coworker interaction must be treated like a clean slate.

This brings me to "the clean slate theory." Every guest or coworker interaction must be treated as a clean slate. For any of us who have worked in the hospitality profession, we all know how common it is to have back-to-back interactions, be it with guests or even with coworkers. We might be in the middle of solving a time-sensitive crisis for a previous guest when a new guest approaches the desk. Understanding the clean slate theory, the hospitality professional must be able to address and interact with the new guest without allowing the emotions from the previous interaction to color this new interaction.

Naturally, this is easier said than done, especially when stakes are high, requests are backing up, and emotions might be heightened. We have to remind ourselves that everything that needs to get done will get done. We also have to become extremely efficient at prioritizing. Not all tasks or requests need to be treated with the same level of urgency and learning to triage your tasks is crucial to being able to efficiently manage your workload.

By keeping things fresh you will set the tone for exceptional service, and tie together all the other pillars of hospitality. If any one of these is slightly off or misses the mark, it provides an incomplete experience. A guest might not even be able to pinpoint where the shortfall may have happened, nor would that be the point because it ultimately is about how we make the guest feel. Each pillar is contingent upon the successful execution of the others. Just as all coworkers must work together to influence the whole guest journey, these pillars also work together to provide an exceptional hospitality experience.

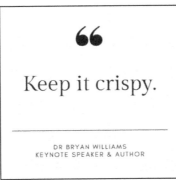

> Keep it crispy.
>
> DR BRYAN WILLIAMS
> KEYNOTE SPEAKER & AUTHOR

❝
Effective communication is the conduit of great service. Communication sets the tone and establishes expectations. It includes what is said as well as what isn't said.

CHAPTER 4

The Art of Effective Communication

What is Effective Communication

First, let us determine what communication is. Simply put, communication is the exchange of information and news. *Effective communication* is the ability to convey information to produce or inspire the intended result or goal. To be truly effective, it encompasses more than just verbal and written skills. Nonverbal communication plays a significant role, oftentimes supporting language and tone. But nonverbal, or physical, cues can also communicate what isn't being said, and can even be more important than the message actually being voiced.

> *On a recent flight, there was a young, handsome flight attendant. He seemed quick and competent, and over the course of the flight, he proved to be as such. An elderly lady was inquiring about being cold on the flight and asked if she could get a blanket. The flight attendant swiftly replied, "Yeah, no. We don't have any blankets." Naturally, the elderly lady was shocked. What major airline doesn't have extra blankets? Of course, this was during the COVID-19 pandemic, and extra items, from magazines to blankets, had been removed. The young flight attendant replied, "Yeah, because there's COVID, we don't have any blankets." In*

fact, his reply was so quick, the elderly lady did not understand him. He had to repeat himself a few times, each time becoming a little firmer.

There were a few things terribly wrong with this interaction. Seeing that the young flight attendant was bright, I just knew if he had had the right guidance, the interaction would have been entirely different.

There was no apology. He may have explained the reasoning behind not having any blankets, but his delivery was curt and matter-of-fact, it lacked warmth. He could have shared a bit of empathy, taken note that the woman was older and slowed his reply, and offered an option to help the situation, even something as simple as turning off her air for her. His language was also casual. Being she was of a different generation; I could see that too rubbed her the wrong way.

All in all, what could have been a pleasant interaction, where the flight attendant could have made a memorable moment, instead caused a moment of discomfort. The elderly lady was made to feel as though she was a nuisance and that her request/comment was not valued. Because of his language and delivery, he arguably made her feel as though he was talking down to her.

Why Communication Matters

Effective communication has the ability to take the guest on an emotional journey. It guides, shapes, and colors their experience. Communication is one of the key components to bridging service and hospitality. And it is with effective communication that humans are able to engage and interact, creating a story of service. That storyline of service is hospitality.

> **❝**
> The guests have positive experiences because of all the magic created behind the scenes. Effective internal communication can change the overall guest experience.
>
> ADAM ISROW
> CO-FOUNDER GOCONCIERGE

Effective communication skills play a significant role in interpersonal relationships. How one communicates, both with verbal and non-verbal skills defines and drives interactions between a hospitality professional and the person with whom they are interacting.

Verbal communication is rooted in clarity that involves speaking slowly and thoughtfully and repeating back the request to ensure the message is clear. Other characteristics include being focused, staying calm, being genuinely interested, displaying the appropriate emotion to a situation, and conveying affirmations. And then affirmations can be done by incorporating statements and phrases such as: "I agree with you, and…" "I understand what you were saying…" "Great job…"

Nonverbal skills include both facial expressions and body language. Each must match the verbal component of the interaction. Steady eye contact, a smile, a pleasant pitch and tone of the voice, professional posture, appropriate proximity to the receiver, and hand gestures should reinforce what is being said and provide feedback to the recipient.

I believe that every guest needs to be treated as if they are the most important person in the hotel every time they have a request. In addition, it is not sufficient to just fulfill the request, the guest's expectations must be met and exceeded at every opportunity. The service should be calm, seamless, and so efficient in its execution that it appears effortless.

JAMES G. LITTLE
CHEF CONCIERGE THE PENINSULA
BEVERLY HILLS

From Warm Welcomes to Fond Farewells and Questions in Between

Communication is so much more than just verbal exchange. One is able to communicate via physical cues, a nod, a hand across the heart, and most simply and effectively, a smile. How we make a guest feel starts the moment they enter the property. We continue to reinforce a sense of welcome, warmth, and comfort in every exchange throughout the duration of the stay. And most importantly, we send guests off with a very fond farewell, with the sentiment that we eagerly await their return.

More than the welcomes and the farewell, all the interactions in between are moments when we can foster relationships. Asking questions is a big part of engaging with guests. Never make an assumption about what a guest wants and needs. Take time to question the guest and get to the root of their request in order to facilitate accurate information and provide alternative solutions. At a minimum, you should ascertain the guest's full name, room number, dates of service, the time associated with the service, specific preferences for any services, and contact information. Ask if it is appropriate to bill the room account or to use the credit card on file for any charges that may apply. Conversely, the same principle applies to any vendor you may be booking services with. Ask as

> The goal has always been about talking to the guest's heart rather than to the guest's mind. It's about the "emotional experience" that a guest has at their property.
>
> SERGE ETHUIN
> GENERAL MANAGER OF THE HOTEL METROPOLE MONTE CARLO

many questions as possible so you can provide the guest with complete information and anticipate any needs they may have. All of this works together to build rapport and communicate effectively.

Delivery Is Everything

We have all had a moment (or five) when we had an interaction with someone that rubbed us the wrong way, usually due to the manner in which the message was delivered. As a hospitality professional, always remember that how we deliver or say something is just as important as the information being shared.

Early in my career while working at the Four Seasons, Washington DC, as a hostess in the restaurant, I had to learn a courteous and polite way to let guests know that we were unable to take their reservation. Instead of saying, "Yeah, sorry, we are full tonight." The proper response was, "My apologies, but we are fully committed. May I put you on the waitlist or assist in making a reservation on another day?"

Of course, the language is formal. Formality of language should be adjusted depending on the brand or business. Formality aside, it was the delivery that painted an emotional arch for the guest. Starting with an apology, there was a sense of empathy. Choosing the words "fully committed" was also a more elegant way of saying "we're booked up." And then, the big win, offering an option at the end turned a "no" into another possibility. At that point, it is up to the guest to decide if that will work for them, but you have presented an alternate solution putting the decision back on the guest, meaning they will be the one to say no, not you.

It is these little nuances that make hospitality a slow psychological dance. And if done deftly, the hospitality professional can make any guest acquiesce to a situation.

Proper Language vs Slang

As with the story shared at the beginning of this chapter, proper language is extremely important. The use of proper language sets the tone for the exchange. Subconsciously, it also gives you a sense of authority and you command a certain level of respect.

You are regarded as well as you speak. They may say clothes don't make the person, but they certainly influence first impressions. The same applies for the language you choose to use.

Choose your words wisely and think about what they imply. It is quite common to say, "no problem." In pop culture language, this is a very casual way of expressing an acknowledgment of a request.

"Can I have a wake-up call at 7 am?"

"No problem!"

Even if delivered in a positive and uplifting tone, if we were to break down semantics, it would imply that there was a problem. A better response would be a slight shift in verbiage to something such as:

"Absolutely, I will take care of that," or, "Certainly, it would be my pleasure."

Thank You, You're Welcome

Always have the last word. Not in a one-upmanship way, but in a way that you "button" or end the interaction. Typically, at the end of an interaction, a guest will say "thank you." A simple "It's my pleasure!" is always a pleasant way to end an exchange. If you would like to take it up a notch, I personally have found that ending a conversation with "thank you" implies that it was indeed *your* pleasure to speak with the guest, be it you took a request, solved a billing issue, or simply had a nice conversation.

Similar to "no problem" implying there is a problem, using "you're welcome" to end an interaction has more of a personal tone. "You're welcome" could also imply that the action or service was a favor. In the world of hospitality, we should strive to make the guests feel like we took pride and joy in assisting them. The goal is to make the guest feel like we genuinely are there to serve. When in doubt, always err on the side of being more professional.

Match Their Style

Often discussed in psychology, research has shown that people who experience the same emotions are likely to develop feelings of connection, understanding, and ultimately trust. Mirroring body language, as well as spoken language, makes people feel understood. And if we have learned anything in understanding hospitality, it is all about making people feel comfortable, welcomed, and acknowledged.

In terms of communication, honing-in on how a guest speaks, from pacing to energy, is an effective way to communicate. You are gauging their comfort level and speaking their language—literally.

There is one exception, and that is changing pace of delivery when de-escalating a conflict. I will discuss that in further detail in a later chapter.

> Hospitality is about connection, not perfection.

CHAPTER 5

The Role of Relationships in Hospitality

Hospitality is All About Relationships

People are the most important part of the hospitality industry. The workplace—be it a restaurant or hotel or be it a beautiful, state-of-the-art property—comes to life through the people employed there. Understanding that people are the fabric of the business, it only makes sense that relationships play an invaluable role in the world of hospitality.

>
> Hospitality is all about relationships. Your relationship with your coworkers, management, guests, and vendors. Positive relationships are imperative to being a successful hospitality professional.

Every interaction a hospitality professional has within their workplace is considered to be a relationship. Some relationships are brief, while others span years. Some relationships include daily communication, and others are defined by interactions every couple of months. The goal is to always have positive interactions. Fostering relationships in the workplace, especially over time, both with guests and coworkers, is critical to a hospitality professional's career success.

Internal vs. External Hospitality

As hospitality is a natural extension of positive relationships, we should look at the concepts of internal and external hospitality (or relationships).

Guests are the distinction between internal and external hospitality. Any hospitality or services that are directed towards and for guests fall under the notion of external hospitality. In the service industry, typically this is where the focus stops—it is *customer* service after all. But to create a truly successful hospitality business or environment in the workplace, it is imperative to focus internally.

Internal hospitality refers to the relationships that happen within the employees of a business. Without question, one of the best ways to ensure an incredible hospitality experience for a guest or customer is to make sure the internal culture of the workplace fosters internal hospitality.

Internal hospitality is how coworkers, managers, and departments interact with each other. As mentioned above, a culture of hospitality sets the tone for external interactions. It also inspires, educates, and leads by example the notion of hospitality. If employees are well taken care of by their management, their coworkers, and even through interactions with other departments, those individuals are continuously reminded of how good it feels to be the recipient of real hospitality, inspiring them to also want to provide that same feeling to guests and customers.

Ritz Carlton is known for their motto, "Ladies and gentlemen serving ladies and gentlemen." This phrase is significant on a number of levels. It is a hospitality twist to "The Golden Rule" that implies that employees and staff should be treated just as well as the actual guests.

One of the simplest ways to demonstrate internal hospitality is by treating internal requests like external requests. Just as one gives attention, care, and focus to a request by a guest, the same respect must be given to colleagues' requests. Of course, where time is a factor, the guest comes first. But ultimately, colleagues must be treated with the same consideration as external guests.

Understanding the Machine

A successful business runs like a fine machine with multiple components and moving parts, all meticulously integrated to ensure everything runs smoothly. In a hospitality business, there are various roles and departments that work together to ultimately operate successfully. Even though each department may have its own set of corporate standards to meet, every department still works together to meet their goals, maintain their standards and create the guest experience.

An Attitude of Willingness and Awareness

To truly understand how the entire business works, it is important to take the time to understand how all the roles, departments, and pieces work together. This means taking the time to learn about departmental operations as well as the individuals working within those departments. By understanding the goals, priorities, and personalities of your team and earning the ins and outs of each department, their proclivities, and idiosyncrasies, you can deduce the strengths and weaknesses of your business and develop effective strategies to increase the overall level of service of the property.

Developing these interdepartmental relationships strengthens not only the sense of community but the significance of the team, working together for a common goal. The best attitude to have is one of willingness and awareness—a willingness to learn, help, and dive in where needed and an awareness of others' strengths, weaknesses, and even pain points. These attitudes are not only humbling, but they create an open environment that cultivates genuine teamwork.

As mentioned before, hospitality is not a one-off interaction, but an entire mentality and experience. You have to have a holistic approach towards hospitality. Think about it: a guest's experience cannot be created by individual silos of service. Too many roles rely on each other. For example, a server can't take an order *and* cook the food *and* clean the dishes *and* seat incoming guests all at once. Roles are important, as is building a foundation where coworkers and colleagues work together to create the guest experience.

> **We are now reaching a point where Millennials are the largest segment in the workplace. In 2020, 50% of the US workforce is made up of Millennials, and it will be 75% by 2030, according to the US Bureau of Labor Statistics.**

In the right environment, it can be easy to create a team bond. Coworkers tend to form these bonds naturally unless there are some major personality clashes. But another area to focus on is management—does management work from a top down, autocratic approach, or is there more of a democratic and inspiring managerial style? A few factors go into managerial approaches, but it would be remiss of me not to talk about the current demographics of the workplace.

Baby Boomers and Millennials often have vastly different views of work, which comes through in how they interact. For one, their values are different. Many Baby Boomers value a steady paycheck and other compensation while Millennials care more about achieving a good work/life balance. Millennials are also very comfortable with technology, expect to use it in the workplace, and are quick to embrace new technology. While Baby Boomers, on the other hand, might be more resistant to change and to adopting new technology into their jobs. Of course, these are gross generalizations, but these differences alone can create friction if Baby Boomers hold "entitled" Millennials in contempt, and Millennials grow increasingly frustrated with "condescending" Boomers.

The Importance of Interpersonal Abilities

Given the social nature of the hospitality industry, the ability to interact successfully and positively with others is of the utmost importance. One's "emotional confidence" often holds more weight than technical skills—this emotional competence marks the difference between a good hospitality professional and a *great* one. From communication to professionalism to knowledge, every element that makes a hospitality professional unique is filtered and funneled through their interpersonal abilities.

>
> The more you move up in an organization, the more you realize it's never about you. Leadership is not about being in charge; it is about the people you are leading. It's really about thinking outside of yourself.
>
> DAN COCKERELL
> FORMER VP OF DISNEY

Can We Be Friends? The Value of Developing Relationships

Every interaction a hospitality professional has within their workplace is considered to be a relationship. Whether brief, established, a unique moment or regular occurrence, the goal is to always have positive interactions. Developing interpersonal relationships in the workplace, especially over time, with both guests and coworkers, is critical to career success for a hospitality professional.

With the guest, a positive relationship is the result of providing quality service. Quality service can be defined as meeting and exceeding guest expectations through an anticipation of needs and creation of wow moments. The basis of a customer service relationship is providing service. If a concierge consistently performs "above and beyond," this positively influences the relationship.

Strong interpersonal relationships with coworkers and vendors create a harmonious workplace filled with contentment and productivity. Coworker relationships create a sense of "teamwork" and help the other coworkers by streamlining productivity within the workplace. With all team members together, they can efficiently service the guests' needs. Vendor relationships, similar to coworker relationships, establish a team effort outside the workplace, reflecting the success of the hospitality professional related to external contacts and linkages.

Relationships don't stop in the workplace. The industry may be large, but the hospitality community is rather small. Mentorship is a critical component to growing a successful career in hospitality. Not only for the mentee, but the mentor can also find a mentorship relationship rewarding. They say to never burn bridges. Mentorships are a fantastic way to build bridges.

> One thing that has helped me a lot during my career is having mentors. I actively sought out the right mentors. The value of networking is so important, and not just when you need something. You'd be surprised at how much people will come to the rescue.
>
> RAUL LEAL
> FORMER CEO OF VIRGIN HOTEL GROUP

Helping Guests Foster Their Own Relationships

Taking the value of relationships, a step further, let us look at it in regard to the guest experience. If your business is able to enrich relationships between your customer/guest and the people your guest cares the most about, then your business will create a life-long customer. This is the most selfless value a business can provide. It goes deeper than just the traditional business-and-guest exchange where typically a business is working *for* a guest. Now through genuine hospitality, you are able to work with the guest, on their side, to make them the hero in their lives.

This deeper exchange transcends the traditional business-to-consumer (B2C) model and builds a rapport and relationship that is far more meaningful.

A few examples we can see today:

In the healthcare industry, the Mayo Clinic changed the design of its buildings and even its furniture to encourage relationships. They built larger rooms for doctor-patient consultations so their families and loved ones can attend, and even installed custom-built furniture that allows everyone to have a seat comfortably.

The Ritz-Carlton Resort at Half Moon Bay in California, as well as a number of other resorts around the world, does more than offer to take photos for families and couples as they enjoy the resort. They go a step further. They print and frame the resulting pictures for guests to take home so they can remember their time together.

DryBar has done exceptionally well in the world of offering quick salon services. But where they take it a step further in helping clients foster their own relationships is directly in their booking process. Through their booking app, guests can invite their girlfriends to join them for their hair blowout appointment. More than building relationships, this is also a great marketing play!

The connections that one can foster in a hotel don't need to be grandiose gestures or even costly services or amenities. Quite often, it all comes down to the simple, thoughtful touches. Guests benefit as much from the subtle actions of attentive employees who turn the music down when they see guests trying to talk, avoid interrupting in the middle of an intimate discussion to ask how the food is, or even offering pet amenities for a guest who is traveling with their furry loved one.

The ultimate form of hospitality is not making it about the property, hotel, or business; it is truly about focusing on the guest. And if you can take it a step further and help a guest deepen their own relationships, it's a win-win.

> Not all requests are possible. Great hospitality is delivering a "no" without actually saying "no."

CHAPTER 6

Culture of Yes, and When to Say No

Starting with a "Can-Do" Mindset

In the world of luxury hotels, it seems many guests have taken Walt Disney's famous quote to heart. As a hotel concierge, I have been asked for an incredible number of things.

> *"Can you arrange for a private magic show in our suite? And if they can do the famous dove and rabbit trick, that would be great!"*
>
> *"I'll get right on it."*
>
> *"Can you help us buy a miniature maltipoo, train it, obtain all the appropriate shots at the vet... and then can you help us get it back to Kuwait?"*
>
> *"Let me look into that."*
>
> *"I don't like traffic. Can you have a helicopter take me to Coachella? We are ready to leave in ten minutes."*
>
> *"Let me make a quick call."*

The requests and stories are vast and elaborate. It is what keeps a true hotelier on their toes. Expect the unexpected, but more than that, always maintain an attitude that it can be done. At the end of the day, any request can be fulfilled. It is then up to the guest to decide to move forward.

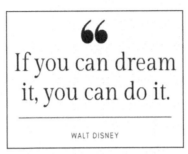

> **If you can dream it, you can do it.**
>
> WALT DISNEY

Yes, and What Is Your Question?

That is the beauty of hospitality, and certainly in the luxury space—yes is always the answer. The next step is figuring out what you just said yes to and then making it happen. Of course, one must always stay calm, cool, and collected, even if on the inside the levels of anxiety are high. Saying yes must not be confused with knowing the answer right away. All too often, those new to hospitality are concerned about knowing all the answers. Of course, knowing the answer can save a few steps in the process of fulfilling a request, but by no means should one be limited to that.

Part of the art of being a concierge at a five-star hotel is being able to accept any request with professionalism and confidence, even if you have no idea how you will accomplish the task. It is always important to get as much information from the requesting guest as possible, as additional questions are inevitable. Keep in mind that you may not be able to fulfill the exact request; however, you may be able to provide a similar experience. The bottom line: there is no guest request that should be handled without the goal of exceeding their expectations.

"It is not about knowing *all* the answers.

It is about knowing how to *find* the answers."

When a guest makes a request that immediately has you in a head spin, the most important thing is to not let them see you sweat. It is a perfectly acceptable answer to say: "You know what, I don't know. But I would be happy to look into it and find out for you."

Knowledge is power, and the more you know and remember, the faster and more reliably you can answer questions and assist with guest requests. Never give guest information if you are not 100% sure it is correct. Offer to research the information and send it to the room so they can review it at their leisure. Never try to lie to a guest and pretend you know what the information is. It is better to be honest and forthcoming.

Pro Tip:

When researching new information or preparing a document with information, always save the document for future reference. Create your own "cheat sheets."

Sharing in the excitement with an eagerness to solve their request indicates that you are on the guest's side. In the chapter "Resolving Conflicts," we will discuss more in-depth the importance of letting the guest know they have been heard. But in this case, expressing your willingness to find out something that you previously did not know lets the guest know that you too value their request. Worst-case scenario: if the options or answers are not favorable, the positive attitude and valiant effort will not go unnoticed.

No... But Always Have Options

A true hospitality professional never actually says no, so essentially, the answer is always yes. Situations may arise where you may not be able to accomplish exactly what the guest requested. When this happens provide alternatives of an equal caliber that are thoughtful and comparable to the original request. Keep in mind comparable time, distance and cost when making additional recommendations.

Options take the request to the next level. Not only is it impressive if you find an answer for a request you previously did not have but offering a guest options to their request demonstrates truly going above and beyond. Options indicate thoughtfulness and thoroughness in research, and they reflect that the request was deemed important.

> The greatest success is having to say no to a guest but they walk away feeling as though you've said yes because of how you've made them feel. It's how you've delivered the information and the way in which you've delivered it that has made them feel accepting and heard and taken care of.
>
> ROBERT MARKS
> CHEF CONCIERGE AND PAST
> PRESIDENT OF LES CLEFS D'OR USA

Options are appreciated by the guest, and they are also useful for yourself. By thinking ahead and procuring several options for a guest, you now minimize the number of times you might have to go back and forth with the guest. It eases the task on you while making you look like a hero.

Guests have a built-in expectation, especially in a five-star environment, that they can get anything they want when they want it. For years, the industry has been built on the mantra of "we don't say no to a guest." As enticing as this concept is, it is just not realistic. At some point, you will be faced with a situation where you cannot accommodate a guest request based on the resources at your disposal or the situational variables that are in play, and you will have to ultimately tell them no.

When that time comes, it's all about how you tell the guest no. You want to be gracious and empathetic in your delivery, but more importantly, you want to offer them alternatives that are as good as or better than what their original request was. There is a firm line in the sand when it comes to illegal or unethical requests. The guests know this yet they may have been indoctrinated into such a pattern of having their requests met that they feel comfortable enough to ask.

No With a Side of Humor

You want to be careful how you answer questions that could blur the line of being illegal or unethical. What has worked for me over the years when being asked for assistance with "companionship" for the evening was to apologize and say, "I just can't guarantee the quality of the experience, so, unfortunately, I can't recommend anything." This usually resulted in a laugh and a smile, which diffused the awkwardness of the moment. Will this work for everything? Absolutely not, but the point here is to use your judgment to craft a response that is specific to the guest you are helping and allows you to say no in such a way that it is completely acceptable and understandable and appreciated for your candor.

James G. Little, Chef Concierge
The Peninsula, Beverly Hills

Taking Ownership

Assuming ownership of each guest interaction, be it a request or a complaint, is imperative in hospitality. Never, ever say to a guest, "That is not my department." When a guest shares feedback or makes a request, from that point forward, it is your request to handle. Of course, this does not translate into literally unclogging their toilet or cooking their steak well-done. It simply means that you are taking ownership to pass on the relevant information to the individual who will execute their request.

In the case of feedback, you must let them know their commentary was taken to heart and passed along to the appropriate department. The best way to communicate this is to pass along the information, and then call or speak with the guest again to let them know you have shared their feedback. By simply saying yes and not circling back to the guest, it does not emphasize that you have done anything with the information they have given you.

How Ethics Plays into Hospitality

In a world where anything goes and yes is always the answer, at what point does one say no? The simplest answer is: So long as it is legal, ethical, and moral, the answer can always be yes. Clear enough, but what if it is a grey area?

Rule of Thumb:

If there is any doubt on the legality, morality, or ethical nature of the request, it is acceptable to deny assistance.

First, we must break down morality and ethics. Morality is the personal distinction between right and wrong. Morals deal with behaviors as well as motives. Although many people often use morals and ethics interchangeably, they are indeed different. Ethics deals with moral principles relating to human behavior. To be ethical is to do what is right according to the standards of a group or culture.

Technicality aside, why is it important for a hospitality professional to make ethical decisions? Actions are always a reflection of something much larger than the person. As a hospitality professional, you represent your hotel, restaurant, or company.

Cultivating and maintaining credibility is a fundamental requirement for success and a positive professional reputation, and thereby, professional prosperity. Credibility is something earned; it takes time, patience, and consistency to build. I have seen all too often where years of professional experience and respect were completely destroyed by a few instances of questionable behavior. Whatever the request, regardless of the perceived benefit, a true hospitality professional must know when to say no.

A single moment of misunderstanding can be so detrimental that it makes us forget a hundred beautiful moments spent together.

How Ethics Plays into Being Genuine & Authentic

At the end of the day, it is imperative that you know your boundaries, know the rules and know your resources. The boundaries are a code of ethics and guidelines put in place by the property or company. The rules include state and local laws, prioritizing guest safety, the property's image, as well as the property's assets. The resources are departments and businesses you can turn to for guidance—think upper management, Human Resources, security, and even external sources like the Better Business Bureau (BBB).

If there is ever a question on the ethical nature of a request or task, always remember to lead by example and act with integrity.

> **Two Rules to Remember:**
>
> *1. Lead by example:*
>
> **Behave in ways that you would want others to behave, either in your position or as a colleague.**
>
> *2. Act with integrity:*
>
> **Always uphold the highest professional standards. Nice guys don't finish last. They sleep better at night.**

The greatest success you can have is this: when you've had to say no to a guest, yet they walk away feeling as though you've said yes because of how you've made them feel. How you've delivered the information and the way in which you've delivered it has made them feel accepted, heard, and taken care of.

All of this to say, have fun finding ways to say yes. Just know the limits. Or as some might say, when to say your safe word... No.

The safe word is always no.

> Your actions not only represent yourself, but they represent your company as well as your profession.

> "Simply put, it is all about positioning and setting yourself up for success. The goal: Turn complaints into memorable moments and manage or redirect expectations."

CHAPTER 7

Conflict Resolution

Conflicts Are Inevitable

Conflicts are inevitable in any business. Where humans interact, conflicts will arise. And as much as you may want to avoid conflicts, the goal is to not only master resolving conflicts but to look at them as opportunities to create life-long customers. Some of the closest relationships I have built with guests and vendors have started because of a conflict resolution. "Turn lemons into lemonade," "every grey cloud has a silver lining." The metaphors and catchphrases are endless because this is a skill that is universal to every profession and walk of life.

> **"** The way in which you approach a conflict says a lot about how it's resolved.
>
> ROBERT MARKS
> CHEF CONCIERGE AND PAST PRESIDENT
> LESS CLEFS D'OR USA

In hospitality, fixing service issues is arguably more important than delivering exceptional service. Guests have come to expect the exceptional. On one hand, it is amazing that we have consistently delivered on such a high level that guests have such high standards. On the other hand, this leaves very little wiggle room for error. And unfortunately, in any human-driven business, errors are bound to happen.

Steps to Resolving Conflicts & Issues

Broken down, here are the key steps to successful conflict resolution.

Listen. Guests always want to be and feel heard. Depending on the situation, sometimes just listening alone is enough to resolve an issue. If it is a more serious matter, or if the guest feels strongly about the problem, listening is just the first step. Listening tells the guest that you are on their side, and you are giving value to their thoughts, opinions, and complaints. Secondly, and important for the astute hospitality professional, a guest will actually share clues as to how they want to resolve the issue. You can begin to piece together a solution by actively listening to the guest.

Most importantly, do not escalate the conflict by adding fuel to the fire and allowing your own emotions to get the better of you **EVEN IF YOU ARE IN THE RIGHT!** Your job here is not to be right; it is to rectify the perceived wrong that the guest is experiencing.

Acknowledge and apologize. Once the guest or customer has relayed their concerns, you must acknowledge and apologize *carefully*. Acknowledging their issues demonstrates that you were actually listening to them, which indicates that you understand them. And remember, a guest ultimately wants to feel understood. Be empathetic and engaged while discussing the situation. Put yourself in the guest's shoes and understand why they are upset, apologize and assure them that their negative experience is not acceptable and that you will do your best to resolve it.

Additionally, one must *carefully* apologize. I specifically chose the word "carefully" because you want to genuinely apologize, but you do not want to accept full responsibility for the situation until a proper investigation has occurred. This is not to say that their issue is not valid—it probably is—but you do not want to apologize in a way that assumes you, your colleague or the business is at fault. (Unless it is, and then, absolutely take full ownership.)

<u>*Determine an acceptable solution.*</u> Based on the degree of the complaint or issue, offer a solution that appropriately reflects the level of inconvenience. Always be sincere in offering solutions, and carefully approach them. Use the considerable resources at your disposal to find a solution that works for the guest. Some conflicts can be resolved with a simple phone call and most just by listening and empathizing.

In some instances, offering a solution can backfire as some cultures find some solutions insulting. For example, offering a round of drinks at the bar when they do not drink, or offering a discount on a room rate when the guest feels it is an exaggerated response. Sincerity is the name of the game here.

> **Service recovery is more than compensation. You have to determine what is the most appropriate solution for that particular guest.**

<u>*The resolution and follow-up.*</u> Once a solution has been agreed upon, it is imperative to act on that resolution in a timely manner. This again signals to the guest or customer that their concern or issue was valued, and that the solution is being genuinely offered (as opposed to being begrudgingly doled out). Take ownership of the solution and follow up with the guest or customer. Allow some time to pass so the guest has hopefully cooled down and the follow-up feels genuine.

Stay in contact with the guest during the process and after to ensure everything was resolved to their satisfaction. This is a key element that is consistently missed in this process and is the lynchpin that turns a conflict into an opportunity. Before you became involved, the guest was frustrated and upset; after you resolved the situation, you followed up and offered future assistance, and now the guest views you as an ally who will always be on their side. You have gained their trust and loyalty for life.

The Art of the Apology

Now that we have broken down the steps to resolving a conflict, it is important to address the art of the apology. It is one thing to go through the motions or the mechanics, checking off the steps one by one. But it is something completely different to artfully, or skillfully, resolve a conflict.

Own the apology. Service recovery is more than compensation; it is the actual apology. Sincerely express that you are sorry for the situation. Be genuine in your apology.

Never make excuses. Making excuses immediately discredits the apology. Avoid words like "if" or "but."

Watch your language. Keep in mind that apologizing is not the same as saying, "I'm sorry." The language is very different and implies different things. An apology shows that you are humble and accept that mistakes happen. Whereas "I'm sorry" can actually seem insincere and dismissive to some guests.

Forgo "forgiveness." Don't ask for forgiveness. This is a business, not a teenage love story. It is a weird word that has so many implications. It's simply not necessary and seems over the top for most situations.

Check your ego. I've often said that I could apologize all day long to people—in fact, I have friends who can attest to the fact that I can do this. Because even though my apology is genuine, it is not personal. I may be taking ownership for an issue that happened in another department, but I am apologizing, in essence, on behalf of the hotel or business. Some people have a hard time apologizing, but in the world of hospitality, ego simply can't be involved.

Timeliness of the apology. Guests expect an apology to be delivered promptly, so responding to a problem as quickly as possible is critical to guest satisfaction.

All these nuances are important to resolving conflicts. As we can see, the interaction is so much more than taking the steps, but there truly is an art to it. Word choice is just as important as tone, as well as timeliness of delivery.

Can You Hear Me Now?

Have you ever called a company to complain about an issue and explained the whole situation, only to be transferred to another department to have to do it all over again? It is the worst! But the time you end up sharing your story for the fourth time, your anger level will likely have risen.

RULE:
Don't ever make guests repeat themselves, in general, but especially when they are upset.

The best solution for this is always in the habit of explaining the entire situation to the person you transfer or hand the guest off to. Similarly, if you are on the receiving end of this, immediately acknowledge that you are aware of the situation and share a few details so that the guest or customer knows that you are already up to speed on the situation.

Turning Angry Clients Into Life-Long Customers

As I mentioned before, the best attitude is one where you embrace the fact that issues are going to happen. Instead of dreading the conflicts, look at them as opportunities to win guests or customers over for life. The way you resolve an issue can actually turn a situation into a highlight of a guest's experience or stay. Sometimes the smooth trips go unremembered. But it is those trips, where something goes completely awry, and someone at the property steps in to save the day that can lead to a most memorable stay. Conflicts can be seen as your hero moments. And everyone wants to be part of a good hero story—be it the hero or the one needing saved.

The key to preventing issues is to start with managing expectations.

Taking it a step further, it is imperative for a property to examine guest complaints. Complaints are invaluable guest feedback. By identifying common complaints or issues, you can note patterns or trends that need to be remedied.

Perhaps you are offering something different, such as complimentary coffee in the lobby bar. As a result, you decide to take coffee machines out of the rooms. But if the guests *expect* coffee machines in the rooms, they aren't going to be impressed by free coffee in the lobby bar. All they see is that there isn't a coffee machine in the room.

Hence, why you have to *manage guest expectations*. In this case, maybe you share signage directing guests to the lobby bar, notate it on their confirmation email, and place a sign in the room where the coffee machine would be. This is a simple issue that could result in a lot of complaints, but by managing the expectations, you can minimize the negative feedback. Even better, if done successfully, the free coffee in the lobby bar can turn into an asset—a feature that all the guests rave about.

66

With the right mindset,
anything is possible.

CHAPTER 8

How to Make the Impossible, Possible

The Magic Mindset

One of the greatest distinctions of luxury hospitality is this ability to deliver the seemingly impossible, thereby, making the impossible, *possible*. As a former concierge, I was completely in the middle of it. Many people would always ask, "What is the secret?" or they'd say, "You must know everything?" Or they even comment, "You have to know everyone!" And the truth is, while I certainly had connections and I certainly know a good deal (I like to say I know a little about a lot), what it all boils down to is having the right attitude. And I learned this very early on in my career.

I became a hotel concierge at a five-star property in the heart of Beverly Hills at the ripe age of 23. Of course, we all have to start somewhere, but if we really think of the magnitude of the position, I was certainly in over my head. I had just moved to Los Angeles, and although I had been exposed to the finer things in life, I was now being approached by the "rich and famous" for my advice on what to do, where to shop, and where to be seen dining. The world was all so new to me. And to be honest, I didn't know a lot of answers at the beginning.

We all know the phrase "fake it until you make it." Well, I didn't do that. As someone who always operates out of a place of honesty (sometimes to a fault), I couldn't pretend to know something I didn't.

What I had that allowed me to succeed in my job really quickly was the right attitude. I knew what questions to ask to minimize the back and forth, and then I dove in to find the answers. I also would put myself in the guest's shoes and ask myself, "If I presented them with this information, would they have enough information to make a decision?" If they asked me a question, I considered if I would be able to answer them and guide them through the next few steps without having to bounce between the vendor and the guest for every single detail.

Over time, my knowledge grew, to the point that people would ask me questions and I could tell them right away what they could expect. I could far more easily manage their expectations within the first few inquiries before going on a wild goose chase to meet the whim of a guest only to find out they'd moved on in a completely different direction. Efficiency at its finest.

In the world of hospitality, there is this enigma around making the impossible possible. In reality, it boils down to some very simple concepts with the right attitude being the foundation of your success. This mindset is fostered by the internal culture of the company and when combined with the right tools creates the magic that is capable of making anything possible.

> And that's what hospitality is, isn't it? It's a little like magic. And that's why what we do is so special.
>
> ROBERT MARKS
> CHEF CONCIERGE AND PAST PRESIDENT OF LES CLEFS D'OR USA

Pyramid of Service

The Pyramid of Service is a concept that was first introduced to me by James Little, Chef Concierge at The Peninsula Beverly Hills. Broken down, it becomes really easy to understand what you need to fulfill a request. Every request requires a combination of three things: time, money, and contacts.

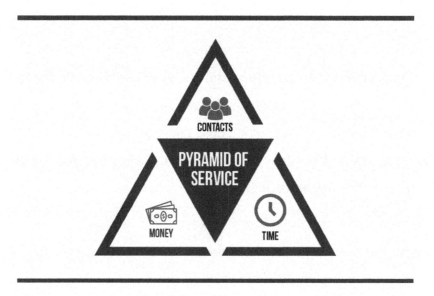

The concept behind the pyramid of service is that virtually anything can be accomplished based on the three pillars of relationships/contacts, money, and time.

With enough money, time, or the right contact, everything is a possibility. The most powerful of the three is contacts or relationships, as this more than anything is often the key to success and is usually the one thing you will have that the guest does not. The more of these three elements you have to work with the greater likelihood you can accomplish any task or request.

You need at least two of the three to pull off a challenging request. With enough time and a reasonable budget, you might not need to have the right connections to fulfill a request. And similarly, if the guest is price-conscious, you will need time and connections to make it happen. Of course, with the right amount of money and connections, you don't need time on your side to pull off the impossible—it's just a quick phone call away.

Scenario 1: Money and Relationships

A guest wants the latest Birkin bag by Hermes, which can be notoriously difficult to get. Hermes never discloses when the bags will be available and in stock in their store. If the guest needs the bag immediately, you lose the benefit of time and have to instead rely on money and relationships to get the bag. If you have a contact at Hermes willing to work with you and the cash on hand to purchase the bag, you can do it. If you have no contact at Hermès, you may still be able to purchase the bag through a personal shopper who has stronger contacts with Hermes; this will force you to focus on the money aspect of the pyramid and pay a higher cost than retail, but you can still get the bag.

Scenario 2: Time and Relationships

A guest wants to plan a special dinner at a very exclusive restaurant that is always booked solid. They are willing to plan their trip around when the reservation can be booked, even if it is six months down the road. This allows you to rely on the benefit of time and put the request in months in advance with the flexibility that works in the restaurant's favor as well as the relationships you have with the maître d'. You don't need to rely on money to make this happen.

Scenario 3: Relationships

A guest wants to go to the same exclusive coastal restaurant that is always booked solid. They make the request on a Friday at 4pm and need the booking that night for 7:30pm. You lose the benefit of time here, and the only way to make this work is if you have a good relationship with the maître d'. Time is no help in this instance, and with the restaurant already sold out, it is unlikely that money will have an effect from the sales perspective, although a lavish gratuity from the guest might help.

Regardless of these tools, it is all about the right attitude. Honestly, with a confident and resourceful mindset, anything is possible. At the end of the day, it is about procuring the option and then leaving it up to the guest to make the final decision.

Of course, this can be the hardest part. After hours or even days, of searching for ways to make a request a reality, within an instant, the situation may change, and the request can be reneged.

>
> My favorite thing about the hospitality industry is the chance to create MAGICAL MOMENTS. These special moments are memories and that guests share and reshare a hundred times over. There aren't a lot of jobs that people can walk away from and say, "I created a memory and an experience that is going to make people smile time and again."
>
> ADAM ISROW, CO-FOUNDER
> GOCONCIERGE

Finding the Fun: Creativity and Imagination

It is important to note that more than having a "can-do" attitude, one should also find joy in challenges, both big and small. As a former concierge, we were presented with wild requests on a regular basis. There is no way that we could know or predict how the day would unfold. As a result, we approached it with an open mind and curiosity, and found enjoyment in embracing anything sent our way.

The way I see it is that you can either choose to sweat the small stuff or you can choose to find the fun. Especially in luxury hotels, requests can be unusual and off-the-wall. If one is stressed over every unusual request, the job will be unbearable. But, if one chooses to "find the fun" in the challenge this tells the guest you are eager to assist, and it makes for a positive experience for both the guest and yourself.

It's not rejection; it's redirection.

Rejection is par for the course. And by rejection, I am referring to figuring out how to solve the request. A true professional doesn't get discouraged by hearing a few no's. In fact, they get creative. After all, we all know there is never one way to get from point A to point B. Mastering this notion is not only an important hospitality skill, but it is an essential life skill. Focus on what works and follow the trail of breadcrumbs leading you to success. Be it at work or in your personal life, the best attitude is to follow the yesses.

> **Opportunities come from connecting the dots. Never give up.**
>
> RUPESH PATEL
> HOTEL OWNER AND INVESTOR

> Five Star service
> is thoughtful.
> It's the unexpected.
> And most of all,
> it appears effortless.

CHAPTER 9

The Tipping Point:
From Four-Star to Five-Star

Four-Star vs Five-Star Service

If we are to talk about four-star and five-star service, most might agree that to be rated as either is an incredible achievement. After all, both are a positive assessment and very impressive. But for those of us striving to be the best that we possibly can be, the nuances between four-star and five-star become extremely significant. After all, how do you measure the difference between great and exceptional?

> **"**
> The difference between four- and five-star service is the thoughtfulness. And in order to be thoughtful, you have to stop thinking about yourself.
>
> HOLLY STIEL
> THANK YOU VERY MUCH INC

Let's first understand the definition of four-star service. four-star service is *great* service. It is honestly a fantastic place to be as a business. You probably have many return customers and an engaged staff, and you pleasantly surprise many guests. A guest will experience many positive interactions, possibly a few unexpected touches, and likely have consistently engaged interactions.

The Tipping Point: What Makes Great Service Excellent

So how do we tip the scales from great four-star service to impressive five-star service?

It first starts with every guest needing to be treated as if they are the most important person in the hotel every time they have a request. It is not sufficient to just fulfill the request; the guest's expectations must be met and exceeded at every opportunity. The service should be calm, seamless, and so efficient in its execution that it appears effortless.

>
> Great service hits the mark everyone is hoping for. Excellent service hits the mark no one knows exists.
>
> ANTHONY MELCHIORRI
> FOUNDER OF ARGEO HOSPITALITY

The second part that needs to be considered is the luxury of time. Five-star service can consist of many things: expensive furnishings, exclusive locations, and well-trained staff with a high staff-to-guest ratio to name a few. But true five-star service delivers one thing consistently, and that is "the luxury of time." Time is the one thing everyone wants more of, and when it is gone, it cannot be replaced. True five-star service gives the guests time to spend on themselves because all their needs are anticipated and taken care of in advance by a true professional. Any task can be accomplished on a guest's behalf, allowing them the luxury of spending more time at the pool, visiting with friends and family, indulging in a spa treatment, or enjoying more romantic time with their partner. If we can take care of all of the day-to-day trivialities and give the guest the opportunity to use their time as they wish, there is no greater luxury.

> **Simply put. Four-star service is solid, reactive service, whereas five-star service is imaginative, proactive service.**

The wow factor is what makes something five-star. But what is the wow factor?

It is the "completely unexpected."

It is the consistent going above-and-beyond.

It is the "yes, and then" attitude.

It is more than anticipating needs. It is being offered something you didn't even know you needed.

It is imaginative, proactive service. Service that is so creative, you would not have thought of it yourself.

It is the story that is created.

> Five-star service *creates stories* that are so memorable, they are told and retold to friends, family, and to anyone willing to listen. Stories immortalize exceptional hospitality.

Let that sink in for a moment.

In many cases, doing your best is going to be enough to get the job done. Delivering five-star service takes extra effort to a new level.

> **❝**
> That's the other big aspect of the tipping point, right? It appears effortless for us. It should always appear effortless.
>
> JAMES G. LITTLE
> CHEF CONCIERGE THE PENINSULA BEVERLY HILLS

One of the goals should be to always enhance a guest's experience by recommending options available to them that would enhance their core request or activity. This extra effort in anticipating the guest's requests and enhancing them is a great way to be a true professional.

Lunch and Then Some

If a guest requests lunch at a hot restaurant, then recommend popular local shopping or perhaps a museum to visit as well (and vice versa).

When offering a wake-up call, also offer a follow-up call, as well as placing a room service order to be delivered at a specific time and even any transportation needs for the morning.

Strong Company Culture

Now that we understand the difference, I am sure you are wondering how, as a business, you can inspire your team to deliver five-star service? First of all, it starts from within. This means that it starts with the culture of the workplace, and it starts with upper management. We have spoken about the Ritz Carlton motto of "Ladies and gentlemen serving ladies and gentlemen," and it absolutely rings true in regard to this. Treat your staff as you would like them to treat the guests. It truly is as simple as that. All of the companies that are known to have the best customer service also have phenomenal and positive company cultures.

>
> Great companies define their values by the behaviors they train their employees. Guests can't observe values or passion, but they can observe their behaviors. They can observe you making eye contact. They can observe you kneeling down to talk to their child. They can observe you being empathetic by asking questions.
> DAN COCKERELL
> FORMER VP OF DISNEY

Some brands you may know, such as Hilton, Kimpton, Hyatt, Marriott, and Four Seasons, all make the list of the best companies to work for. The common thread in all of these, aside from being hospitality companies, is they all have strong corporate cultures that support their employees. After all, a supported employee is a happy employee. And a happy employee extends that attitude towards guests. So when I talk about "hospitality from within," it is so much more than from within a person, but it is also inspired from within a company, working from the inside out.

Technically speaking, in a five-star establishment, there is a higher ratio of staff to guests. So if you are truly looking to commit to a higher level of service and hostility, you must be willing to hire more staff. Also, give your staff greater responsibility and opportunities to independently make decisions to create wow moments. By providing staff with the authority to make certain decisions, without having to run every idea by upper management, they will take pride in the service they provide.

Excellence is not an act; it is consistently exceeding expectations.

Once all the pieces are in place, the staff is of the right mindset, and there are specific goals to provide five-star service, then comes the consistency which we discussed in an earlier chapter. Four-star service might be excellent some of the time, but five-star service is consistently excellent.

ALL. THE. TIME.

Implementing technology into hospitality isn't intended to replace human interactions. It is meant to streamline service, making service more efficient and frictionless.

CHAPTER 10

Personalized Service in a Digital World

Understanding Hospitality Technology

From modern hospitality, we see the birth of hospitality technology, which was and is the ultimate game-changer. Although we often think of the big advances in hospitality tech as being relevant in more recent years, it has in fact influenced the industry for over a hundred years. From in-room radios to the widespread use of credit cards to the internet, many technological milestones have influenced the hospitality industry throughout the 20th and now 21st centuries.

Yet, as it has always been, implementing new technology into the world of hospitality has always been met with skepticism and significant push-back. Change is always scary. Especially when one is looking at the well-oiled machine like a hotel or other hospitality business. One slight change could be a spoke in the wheel.

But imagine, one slight technological enhancement could also make incredible improvements.

The Evolution of Hospitality Tech

Hospitality technology has come a long way over the years, and every development has moved the industry forward in one way or another. Although we often think of hospitality tech more on the consumer-facing front, it is also important to understand how hospitality works from a B2B, or business-to-business, perspective.

Let's take a look at the graphic on the following pages for a timeline of major technological milestones in hotels so we can better understand the evolution of the industry thus far.

KEY DATES OF
TECHNOLOGY IN HOTELS

1894
First in-room telephones (The Netherland Hotel, NYC)

1904
First hotel to offer controlled heating and cooling in-room (St. Regis, NYC)

1920
First in-room bathrooms (The Goring Hotel, London) AND electricity begins to become widely prevalent in hotels.

1927
First in-room guest radios (Boston Park Plaza Hotel, Boston)

1930S
Introduction of hotel room service (Waldorf Astoria, NYC) and popularity of "baby-cages" being attached to hotel room windows.

1947
The Roosevelt Hotel NYC installed TVs in guestrooms and the Westin established the first hotel reservation system.

1950S
RFirst central air conditioner (Adolphus Hotel, Dallas) and the introduction of "Magic Fingers," aka the vibrating bed, grew in popularity.

1958
Sheraton introduces Reservatron, the first automated electronic reservation system in hospitality, and the first toll-free reservation phone number.

1966
InterContinental Hotels & Resorts introduces ice and vending machines in guest corridors.

1969
Westin becomes the first chain to implement 24-hour room service.

1973
TThe Sheraton, Anaheim, is the first to offer free in-room movies.

1974
First guestroom minibars (Hilton, Hong Kong).
* These led to a 500% increase in-room service drink sales.

1976
Two Florida hotels are the first to offer HBO in guest rooms. A year later Showtime and The Movie Channel debuted in hotels as well.

1982
Teledex invents the very first hotel telephone.

KEY DATES OF
TECHNOLOGY IN HOTELS

1983
Westin is the first to offer reservations and checkout using a major credit card. VingCard invents the optical electronic key card.

1986
Teledex introduces the first telephone made specifically for hotel guestrooms.

1994
The first hotel chains launch websites on the Internet (Hyatt and Promus Hotel Corp). This is also when the first online hotel catalog debuted, Travelweb.com. Teledex places the first fax machines in hotels.

1995
Choice Hotels and Holiday Inn are the first to introduce online booking capabilities.

2003
Wi-Fi becomes available in over 6,000 hotels worldwide.

2007
Teledex was the first to introduce touch screen telephones for the hospitality industry with the Teledex iPhone™ (now known as I Series) HD Series and LD Series.

2009
First hotel service app developed for guest service on smartphones (Intelity).

2010
First iPads installed in hotel rooms (The Plaza Hotel, NYC).

2012
First integrated and service-enabled mobile app for an entire hotel brand (Conrad Hotels & Resorts).

2014
Guest room keyless technology is first introduced.

2015
Hyatt uses Messenger to interact with guests.

2016
The world's first robot hotel opens in Japan (Henn-na Hotel), furthering the discussion of automation within hospitality technology.

Today's Biggest Challenges

In today's world, where everyone is living on their cellphones, tablets, and laptops, it's impossible to provide modern service without incorporating technology. Doing so would be completely archaic and not relevant to how we operate as a culture. This being said, the intersection of technology and hospitality has been a point of contention for many years. After all, the essence of hospitality is so rooted in human interaction that it begs the question, how do you maintain a certain level of hospitality in an increasingly technological world?

>
> When it comes to providing seamless service, it is important to balance technology with the human touch to ensure there is always a personal connection.
> ADAM ISROW
> CO-FOUNDER GOCONCIERGE

Simple. Use technology as a tool for efficiency, to provide value and use, and to enhance your hospitality offerings. Technology should not be a scary thing in the world of hospitality, but instead, embraced and heralded for how it allows the industry to evolve. Evolution is the exciting part of any industry. Certainly, it can be scary and most definitely challenging, but as I have always said, you have much to learn from the things that threaten you the most.

For example, the emergence of Airbnb posed a big threat to many hotel companies. There was such an aversion to Airbnb and to what it represented. Very few hoteliers embraced it. I found it exciting. Yes, could the rise of Airbnb take away heads in beds from hotels?

Sure. But I was excited about what Airbnb was doing to evolve travel. First of all, it made travel more accessible by providing lodging options for more individuals, be it driven by more budget-conscious travelers or those looking for long-term options or those traveling as families. These travelers still liked hotels. It just may not have been the best option for this particular trip. So in this case, now hotels could look to expand their other offerings, experiences like high tea service, pool cabana rentals, rooftop cocktails. It was a simple mindset shift that, for those hoteliers who embraced it, allowed certain hotels to really succeed and take advantage of appealing to travelers as more than just a place to rest their heads—but an actual destination in and of itself. Brownie points for those hotels and restaurants that tapped into building "Instagram-worthy" elements into their businesses to truly let guests do their marketing for them.

High Tech While Remaining High Touch

Let's dive into the big challenge that businesses find when wanting to remain high touch in an increasingly high-tech world. Ultimately, it comes down to how you communicate. Whether it is on the phone, via email, text message, or even through social media, each and every one of these communications serves as a "virtual" touchpoint.

So how do you even begin to approach it? Take your in-person standards and create a new set of best practices that are applicable and most importantly, relevant.

Three simple rules:

1. *Anticipate Their Needs.* Yes, this again. Certainly, a pillar in hospitality, but when it comes to communicating in modern forms, it is best to anticipate the information the guest might need. Extra useful information can go a long way to showing that extra care has been taken in their communication.

2. *Use Positive Language.* Written language is very different from verbal communication, and one needs to be very intentional and careful with word choices. Tone is set by vocabulary and punctuation. And most significant, anything that is written can be used against you! So be very careful in word choice, as once it is sent, it exists forever.

3. *Err on the Side of Formality.* As every guest is influenced by their language, culture, and unique upbringing, it is always best to err on the side of formality. Not everyone understands abbreviations, slang, or even colloquial phrases. My rule of thumb is to write as though you are communicating with a grandparent or someone of a significantly different generation. Just because the means of communication may be more casual, it does not mean that how one communicates should be anything less than professional. Casual rapport needs to be earned.

Use Technology to Do the Heavy Lifting

If there is anything that hospitality companies can learn from tech companies, it is all about efficiency. Use technology to do the heavy lifting, such as AI-powered texting services. Services that text with guests and can answer the common questions about a property (i.e., the opening hours of the pool or gym) and can pass along requests, such as extra pillows to housekeeping. In this case, AI-powered services are deployed to increase efficiency and work with your employees. While technological tools tend to the mundane tasks, your employees can focus on connecting with guests, providing that which only humans can really provide—critical thinking, creativity, empathy, consideration, and establish trust and connection with guests.

Technology should be used to tackle not only mundane tasks but to also inspire your employees to feel more empowered to connect with guests. Instead of being buried in smaller tasks and constant questions, your employees can free up some of their time to forge these authentic connections and have genuine interactions.

Ultimately, efficiency is the name of the game. We live in a time where we are used to receiving an immediate response to both inquiries and requests. Focus on implementing certain technology programs to help streamline the guest experience without sacrificing quality.

Naturally, as our world evolves and our relationship to technology expands, so will its role in hospitality. Mobile check-ins and keyless entries have become increasingly popular. But many guests still crave that human interaction, even if it is to complain, inquire about an upgrade, or find out where the best hole-in-the-wall Thai restaurant is located.

The art is to know how to seamlessly incorporate technology while delivering excellent service. It is a fine dance between efficiency and creating genuine connections with your guests.

As the pace of change in our world accelerates with generational transformations and technological advances, these should remain mere enablers as we must stand our ground and reaffirm our beliefs and values that nothing will ever replace our humanity.

TALAL YOUSIF
EXECUTIVE HOSPITALITY ADVISOR

"

Small acts,
when multiplied
by billions of people,
can transform
the world.

CHAPTER 11

Conclusion

Conclusion

One of my most memorable hospitality moments occurred while traveling in Cabo San Lucas and happened to do a site visit at the One and Only Palmilla. Even though I wasn't staying there, I noticed something very unique about all the employees. Of course, they all were expertly trained to pause or step to the side when a guest was in their presence, as well as greet and acknowledge guests through eye contact, a smile, and a nod. This is very common at luxury properties and oftentimes expected. The small gesture that caught my attention was that every employee put their hand over their heart.

The employees did not have to say a word. Their body language said it all. The simple gesture of the hand over the heart encompassed everything I knew about hospitality. Their actions directly reflected that hospitality comes from the heart.

Since then, I have seen the hand over the heart gesture in a number of other properties. Personally, I love how something so simple can have such meaning. And interestingly enough, as stunning as the property was, the interaction with the employees is what made the biggest impact during my short visit.

When we think of high-end, hospitality experiences, we often think of fine linens, exquisite cuisine, incredibly luxurious accommodations. But so much more than all the physical characteristics of a property, it is the employees, the *people*, who really make a hospitality business successful. The "soft experiences" are the tipping point between three, four, and five-star service. The human component is necessary for travelers, consumers, and guests to emotionally connect with the experience.

Consumers are smarter and more knowledgeable than ever. With so much information at our fingertips, we can sniff out inauthentic interactions. Even with the prevalence of social media, which digitally connects people across cultures and geographical locations. Those individuals and businesses who have the most success focus on forging real connections, creating real experiences, and ultimately, making real memories. This notion of "real" truly boils down to being human.

> The future of the luxury travel experience is the "emotional experience." An experience cannot be taught; it must be lived.
>
> SERGE ETHUIN
> GENERAL MANAGER OF THE HOTEL METROPOLE, MONTE CARLO

Regardless of the business you are in, the human element must always be considered. Technology, for example, may positively impact efficiency and create frictionless transactions in terms of delivering a service. Speed and ease are certainly valued by the consumer, but we, as a society, thrive off of human connection. True hospitality, real exchanges, and memorable experiences stem directly from human interaction.

At the end of the day, true, authentic hospitality comes from within—within the employee *and* within the company. The beauty of hospitality is that it is such an integral part of human nature. We, as humans, *want* to care for others and be hospitable. Being of service not only makes us feel good, but it gives us a sense of *purpose*.

This notion of service does not have to be a grand gesture. It can start at home, in your community, with your friends. Leading by example, we can inspire those around us to embrace hospitality in our daily lives. By practicing your skills of empathy and listening, you can make people feel seen, heard, understood, and ultimately valued leading to the formation of genuine connections.

Passion, empathy, and a delight in being of service to others—this is the essence of hospitality. Heartfelt service empowers you to create memorable experiences and positively affect every person you touch and serve. True hospitality starts with you... from within.

> **❝**
> The beauty of hospitality is knowing the impact it can have. One simple gesture can do more than elicit a smile, it has the power to inspire someone to pay it forward. Like throwing a stone into a pond and watching the ripples.
>
> JEFF KULEK
> AREA PRESIDENT AND GENERAL MANAGER
> OF THE LONDON WEST HOLLYWOOD

Stories immortalize
exceptional service.
They bring hospitality to life,
going beyond description
and turning it into
a visceral feeling.

CHAPTER 12

Stories from Behind the Desk

I couldn't end this book without sharing *real* stories and examples of *hospitality from within*. I am admittedly biased, but I do believe that hotel concierges have the most opportunities for creating magical moments for guests. While I have a few special stories, I called upon some of my colleagues from around the world to share their experiences as well. Since hospitality is a team effort, it can't be shared through the lens of one person. Like a stained-glass window, all the colors work together to create a beautiful picture.

How did I form all these connections around the globe? Simply put, it was through the incredible organization of Les Clefs d'Or. Becoming a member not only elevated my commitment to the profession, but it introduced me to the best professionals in the industry. I will forever be proud to call them colleagues, but more so, friends and family.

All of the stories highlight incredibly thoughtful service inspired by the desire and vested interest in crafting a moment that is best for the guest. These stories not only reflect the true spirit of hospitality, but you will notice that many of these memories include how the individual was able to save the day or play an instrumental role in a highly personal moment in a guest's life. Few professions can have such a profound impact on the life of another. And how lucky are we that we get to do just that?

Phone a Friend

Back in 1992, when I was working in my hometown of London, England, I received a phone call from a Les Clefs d'Or colleague from the Park Hyatt Chicago. He explained he had the British Prime Minister staying with him over the weekend (as a concierge, I will not divulge her name). She was an avid Horse Race Fan, and during her weekend in Chicago, a famous British race was taking place. He asked to find out if the race was going to be broadcast in the USA. After speaking to the BBC, they advised me the race would not be televised in the USA. Putting my "thinking cap" on, I came up with a plan. I taped the race on a "video tape," and managed to get it to DHL in time for the tape to be delivered the next morning to my colleague in Chicago. He then arranged for a VCR to be delivered at the same time as her breakfast, and *presto!* With the help of Clefs d'Or, she managed to see the race! This is what we do!

Robert Watson, Chef Concierge,
The Willard Intercontinental, Washington, DC

Bringing Millie Home

While by the concierge desk, my general manager was speaking to a guest who was living in the hotel while her new home was being built in Beverly Hills. She recently lost her husband and was in a deep state of grief and decided she needed her dog "Millie" from her home in London to help her through the process. She requested a private jet for the transport, but knowing the cost would be prohibitive, I casually mentioned I would be happy to fly over commercial, pick Millie up and bring her to Beverly Hills. After spending a week in London getting to know Millie, we headed to Heathrow only to find that the previously agreed-upon dog carrier was too large for the cabin. Millie would have to ride in the cargo hold. This is where the years of customer service came into play as I requested to speak with a supervisor and pointed out that all these arrangements had been made in advance according to the airlines' recommendations, and that being a service professional myself, I expected them to honor their original agreement. After escalating the issue to the head of Animal Quarantine for Heathrow Airport, he decided to allow Millie to ride in the cabin. The airline then upgraded us for the flight. Eleven hours later, we landed at LAX. After a swift ride to the hotel, we reunited Millie with her owner, who greeted her with tears of joy on the front drive. I was able to ease a widow's grief, experience London for the first time, and cement her loyalty and gratitude to the hotel, making the whole adventure a "win" for everyone involved.

James G. Little, Chef Concierge
The Peninsula Beverly Hills

Love Is in the Air

A celebrity guest was in Berlin doing promotions. His wife had stayed home and their anniversary was coming up. A handwritten poem needed to be in America within 24 hours. All courier services were not able to deliver accordingly, so we decided to deliver it ourselves. One of our team members flew from Berlin to Los Angeles, handed over the poem personally and flew back the same day. After working an eight-hour shift, my colleague and I went to his apartment to pick up a toothbrush and his passport. Then we drove straight to the airport and he hopped on a flight to LA. He was probably up for 50 hours. Needless to say the guest was blown away by this extra step to save his anniversary surprise.

Thomas Munko, Chief Concierge
The Ritz-Carlton, Berlin

Origami Paper Cranes

We had frequent repeat guests who would spend their anniversary every year with us. In anticipation of their return stay to celebrate their 38th wedding anniversary, I wanted to do something more unique to commemorate this incredible milestone. In my culture, it is traditionally believed that if one folded 1,000 origami paper cranes, one's wishes would come true. Origami paper cranes are a symbol of hope and at times of healing. I decided to fold 38 origami paper cranes and string them together as a decorative piece to their amenity prior to their arrival. Ornately folded in a variety of beautiful colours and patterns, my hope was that they would continue to celebrate this incredible milestone with us and present it as a token of appreciation for always choosing our property to celebrate it in. The guests were blown away; I was so touched to hear that they now keep the cranes on the mantle of their home. Every year they visit, I fold them a new origami paper crane to add to the piece on the mantle as a new-found tradition we have when we welcome them to the hotel.

Risa Miyake
Fairmont Gold Concierge & Supervisor, Vancouver, BC

Wedding Dress Debacle

We had a bride who was going to have her wedding ceremony that evening. When the maid of honor went to pick up the gown that morning, she found out the store was closed on Sundays. So we went through a couple of different options. What could we do? We thought we could find another store that was open where she could get a similar gown, but this wasn't acceptable to the bride. When we went to the store, we noticed at the bottom of the door a security placard that gave the name of the security company that monitored the store. There was also a telephone number, so we called the security company. They were able to get in touch with the owner of the store, who was then able to come to the store, open it up, and get the wedding gown for the guest so the wedding could go on without a hitch.

Robert Marks
Chef Concierge and Past President of Les Clefs d'Or USA

25th Wedding Anniversary Celebration:
"Something About the Way They Met"

During my tenure as chef concierge at Boca Raton Resort & Club, a couple celebrating their 25th wedding anniversary asked me to re-create and stage the way they met, though in a more luxurious way. On the day of their anniversary, they both dressed in formal attire, he in black tie and she in an elaborate ball gown. On the side of the historic cloister in an open garden, I arranged for a pony, a corral, a pony hand to pull the pony around the corral, a videographer, a butler dressed formally in tails with a silver tray, and champagne for two on ice. As the elegant couple arrived at the corral, the husband placed the wife on the pony as the hand pulled her around the corral. The butler then approached both, serving them champagne, all of which was filmed by the videographer. Apparently, they met at a pony ride and wanted to recreate the entire staging but 25 years later in a much more prosperous and luxurious setting.

Michael Romei, Chef Concierge
The Faena Hotel & Resort, Miami Beach, FL

Creating Magical Moments

A guest was requesting a last-minute invitation to the Magic Castle in Los Angeles for his anniversary. For those who know, the Magic Castle is a members-only, magic and dinner experience. It was a holiday weekend, and there was no way to get the guest in. Wanting to make sure the guest had an option, I suggested, "What if we bring the magic to you and find a magician to perform in your room?" The guest loved the idea! So off I went to research magicians to see what I could pull off. I called and vetted at least ten magicians to see who the most appropriate act for the guest would be. And believe me, it becomes really unusual when you are going into details about magic shows—illusions, mentalism, sleight-of-hand! I presented the options to the guest, which he loved! I couldn't help but giggle when I had to ask my General Manager for approval to have both a bunny and a dove in the room. We were a pet-friendly hotel, but bunnies and doves are a little different than dogs! To this day, this has been one of my most "magical" moments!

Sarah Dandashy, Former Head Concierge
London West Hollywood at Beverly Hills

London - Paris Proposal

Growing up in Canada, I had never heard of a concierge, so I was delighted when I found this amazing role in the hotel where I could make a difference in every guest's stay. I transferred to the concierge desk about a year after starting and loved it instantly. The first week I started, I received an email from a gentleman in Canada who asked for help planning his proposal. Not only was this to start in Canada, but to be spread across London and Paris. I was brand new to the role, but I was hooked and dove right in. We planned for a car to pick up his girlfriend at work in Toronto and to take her to the airport where he was waiting. When they landed in London, there was a car waiting to bring them to the hotel. I'd given them an upgrade to a suite, with chocolates and flowers and access to our Club Lounge. They had a couple of amazing days in London, planned to the minute with visits to the best restaurants, theatres and galleries. I sent them off to Paris where I had arranged a river cruise and dinner at the restaurant in the Eiffel Tower where he proposed.

It was magical, and I remember being so proud that I could be part of something so special. This is what started my love for being concierge, keeping in mind I was brand new and had zero contacts, I don't know how I pulled it off. I'd also never been to Paris, so it was a true miracle! These are the moments we live for as concierge, making amazing memories people will remember forever.

Alixandra Mellor, Head Concierge
Charlotte Street Hotel, London, England

My Dear Friend Steven

While my colleague Paco and I were working on the desk, we received the visit of a new guest looking for something special to do and visit while he and her partner were in town. We got deep into a conversation and realized that Steven, the guest, was a well-versed and knowledgeable in flamenco and Spanish guitar. Paco and I were from Andalucia where flamenco was born, so we grew up with it.

So, we planned their night with a special guitar concert in a tiny little church, Iglesia del Pi, and a dinner afterwards in a gastro tapas bar.

While they were outside, we decided to surprise them upon their return to the hotel. During our conversation, we mentioned a specific Spanish guitarist, Diego del Morao. We decided to purchase the last LP in Barcelona of the guitarist, added a pink fan for her, and a handwritten note. Then we left everything in their room.

They came back, saying hello on their way up to their room. Moments after, they came down to the desk. He was crying, excited and surprised by the special gift. Funny fact: he also thanked us that the fan was pink because he had just bought his partner an entire pink collection of an expensive brand in Paris.

After that, we see them every year and have developed a lovely friendship. We even coordinated a trip Cordoba, and now my next trip will be to his hometown, Taiwan.

Claudio "Klaus" Heldt, Concierge Supervisor
Mandarin Oriental, Barcelona

Misplaced Wallet

We had a guest in town for a conference who then departed the hotel early via taxi, en-route to YVR Airport. Shortly after he departed, he called the Concierge Level to see if we had discovered a wallet left behind in the lounge. I quickly searched the premises and his recently departed room, to no avail. Upon advising the guest, he mentioned that he was circling back to the hotel to retrace his steps. Aware he had no funds on his person, I notified the doorman to expect his return and to provide the taxi driver with a voucher to take care of his trip. Concerned and in anticipation of the worst-case scenario, I gathered some pastries and snacks from our lounge and packaged them up in concern that our recently departed guest would have no funds to eat, as he was connecting flights back to Europe. I quickly wrote another taxi voucher to ensure he wouldn't have to worry about transportation and gave $20 of my own money as a gesture in hopes he would make it home safely with some means. While we were unable to locate it prior to his departure, I gave him my business card and asked that he reach out to us once he arrived home safely. He responded in gratitude, thanking us for going beyond the call in an incredibly stressful situation. Thankfully, someone at the convention centre had turned in his wallet and had arranged to have it shipped back to him. What would normally have been a frustrating end to his visit with us became an experience where he felt grateful to us for ensuring his safe return home.

Risa Miyake,
Fairmont Gold Concierge & Supervisor, Vancouver, BC

Excuse Me, I'd Like a Seat for a Teddy Bear…

I had a guest reach out to me as she was arranging her husband's 80th birthday stay. They were coming from Switzerland and sparing no expense. We organised some incredible things for them, such as a private capsule on the London Eye, a test drive of an incredible vintage car and a helicopter tour of London. It was all pretty standard, until she nonchalantly mentioned that they would have a third passenger on the helicopter: her bear. It turned out she travelled with two teddy bears, one small bear who fit into her purse (she actually carried it around within her cleavage most of the time) and another three-foot bear who couldn't possibly be left at home. These bears were seasoned international travelers. I contacted the helicopter company and asked them if they would be able to have the bear join them. They were happy to accommodate but due to the size of it, they required it to have its own seat. The guests were thrilled, and they ended up having a wonderful time on the helicopter tour, and the 80th birthday celebration was a huge success!

Alixandra Mellor, Head Concierge
Charlotte Street Hotel, London, England

Show of a Lifetime - Grand Ole Opry

An elderly couple sat down at the concierge desk to ask for directions to the Grand Ole Opry radio show in Nashville. They had listened to the show together every Saturday night for 50 years. The couple had saved their money for decades to stay in a hotel as nice as the one on their honeymoon, when they had attended the live radio show. They had no idea tickets were required. Of course, that particular Saturday show the couple was hoping to just walk into happened to be featuring Carrie Underwood as well as a few other big-name artists. All were set to perform for The Opry in an intimate 4400-seat venue, and they typically sell out entire arenas. As you can imagine, the show had been sold out for weeks.

Using years' worth of connections built with the Opry and adding a little patience, some luck, and concierge magic, artist tickets were secured for them to attend the show and to stay within their budget.

It was an experience they waited on for decades, and a memory was created they will never forget.

Laura Cunningham, Former Chef Concierge Nashville, Concierge in Philadelphia, Member Les Clefs d'Or

It Happened During the Day….

When I arrived to work for my overnight shift at the Four Seasons, Austin, at the start of my career, my first call was from a guest who had left his newspapers on the bed when he left for the day. Upon returning, the room had been cleaned and all his newspapers had been thrown away; there were articles that he'd specifically highlighted for further reading. After apologizing for the inadvertent mishap, I could feel the sadness in the guest's voice. Shortly after disconnecting from the call, I remembered housekeeping collected the trash from each room, place it into its own plastic bag, labeled with the room number, before tossing it in the dumpster. My next stop: the compactor room!

Luckily, the overnight steward had not started compacting. So I went on a dumpster dive to find the trash from this guest's room. And yes, it was at the bottom of the bin! Once I had the bag and opened it, the newspapers were all there with articles circled and highlighted in pristine order. I took the newspapers and placed them in an envelope with a note that simply read, "We thank you for staying with us at the Four Seasons, Austin, and regret the inconvenience. Sincerely, Maurice/Concierge."

The next day, there was a letter from the owner and CEO of Four Seasons Hotels & Resort saying thank you for saving the day with a guest comment card written by the guest. That simple act later recognized me as Employee of the Month.

Maurice Dancer, Chef Concierge
The Pierre, a Taj Hotel

Crossing Paths with a Movie Star at 1:00 am

I was working at night at the concierge department. At 1:00 am, a group of people came to the hotel without a reservation. One lady was crying.

I left the desk and came to the lady, and when I was near her, I realized that she was a celebrity from Hollywood. Marisa Tomei was upset because Discovery Channel hired her for a shooting and they chose a hotel near my hotel that Marisa didn't like, and she was upset with that and tired and far away from the USA.

So my first word was, "Welcome, Marisa!" She was surprised that I had recognized her. She asked, "Do you know who I am?" I said, "Of course, Marisa, how can I forget your role in *My Cousin Vinny* the movie. You won an Oscar, and you were fantastic in it. So, let me help you, and please don't cry because you are with the best hands in Buenos Aires." The entire group was happy because I fixed Marisa's problem. She wanted the best hotel in Buenos Aires, and she finally found it and met the concierge who took care of her stay in Buenos Aires.

Maria Esperanza Coarasa, Concierge
Alvear Palace Hotel, Buenos Aires, Argentina

The World's Most-Traveled Buttons

Angela, a concierge from Jakarta, contacted me to do the impossible. A guest of hers had damaged his special vest, which had been tailor made with buttons, and as much as she tried to find a duplicate in all the Singapore stores, she wasn't successful. The jacket was from Massimo Dutti, which is a Spanish brand.

I checked with the stores near me and found 10 buttons, which they were willing to give me at no cost. They took two weeks to arrive at the store, but I had found them.

The next step was the delivery. Naturally, sending these buttons to Jakarta could have proven to be challenging. But magic happened! The buttons arrived the day before I was leaving for Cannes to attend the big international Les Clefs d'Or congress (conference). I was able to take them with me to the congress and hand deliver the buttons to the President of Les Clefs d'Or Singapore. These might be some of the world's most-traveled buttons as they made it from Barcelona to Jarkarta by way of Cannes, Paris, and Singapore! But ultimately, Angela was able to receive them and surprise her guest.

This was only possible thanks to our association where the ultimate goal is always to make our guests happy.

Claudio "Klaus" Heldt, Concierge Supervisor
Mandarin Oriental, Barcelona

Needle in a Haystack

One day, I had a guest of mine approach the desk in a complete panic! When he had flown into LAX, he decided to leave his expensive road bike in storage. The problem was it was now two weeks later, and he had lost his claim ticket and couldn't remember the name of the storage facility. All he could remember was that it was located near LAX, and he gave his bike to an employee named José. Well, in Los Angeles, that doesn't narrow things down too much! Through a series of questions I was able to figure out what airline he came in, miraculously spoke to someone in baggage claim for that airline, and after two more phone calls, I found the storage unit, José, AND the bike! Needless to say, this was a needle in a haystack experience!

Sarah Dandashy, Former Head Concierge
London West Hollywood at Beverly Hills

Christmas on Ice

The week of Christmas is extremely busy for all our teams at the Fairmont Banff Springs. Our "Castle in the Rockies" has over 700 rooms and close to 2000 people all wanting to make the perfect Christmas memories. In VIP concierge, we have multiple guest requests going on at any given moment throughout the day, and during this week, we barely have time to answer the phone.

It was Friday afternoon, two days before Christmas, and I had a guest who had left a message with a colleague saying he wanted to get an ice sculpture. As he was staying in our royal suite, my initial thought was that he wanted to have family and friends up to his room and have a small ice sculpture as a centerpiece.

When I could finally find a moment, I called the guest back and asked him what size he was looking for, knowing full well that the smallest size needs at least a week in advance to order (and that is considered a rush order). Well, he didn't want a small one; he wanted a huge one, as big as he could get! He wanted to have his family name on top in big letters and then *Merry Christmas* written underneath. Of course, being a concierge as long as I have, I never want to say no, and I always want to make the impossible happen for my guests. This time, I thought I had met my match. What made it so impossible was we had three days to have it made and put in place, two of those days were Christmas Eve and Christmas Day, and the closest ice sculpture company was a 2-hour drive.

I worked every angle and contact I had, and with a little extra coercion of a 4-course meal and the promise of a bottle of wine in our Signature

1888 Chop House restaurant, I was able to get the company to agree to make the sculpture.

Next, I had to find an appropriate place on our property where I could place an 8-foot-wide sculpture, and not take away from the holiday experience from our other families and guests visiting. After a quick walk around the property with my general manager (in our suits in minus-20-degree weather), we found the perfect spot to have the sculpture placed. If it wasn't already hard enough, my guest then added the following: Requests for individual square foot cubes of ice with all his children and grandchildren's names carved inside for a 3-D effect, a fire pit with benches to sit outside and enjoy, for the words *Merry Christmas* to have red lettering, and of course special lighting for the ice sculpture to light it up at night (no big deal when all the outdoor power on the patio is turned off for the winter!).

We made it all come together for our guests, and of course, we made sure that they all went outside with fresh hot chocolate, including shaved chocolate, marshmallows, and fresh whipped cream.

This has been one of my favourite requests. It felt great making the impossible possible, and as a bonus, to give Gibson's Whiskey some free advertising as so many other guests got to see the end result.

Don Mooney, VIP Concierge,
The Fairmont Banff Springs

Proposals 'R' Us

One of the great privileges of being a hotel concierge is sharing everything from profound losses to some of life's great celebrations with our guests. After all, all aspects of life happen in a hotel. Sometimes we are privileged to be able to add just a bit of assistance and concierge magic to the memorable occasions. One of my greatest pleasures over the years is to have assisted many gentlemen and one lady to prepare to ask the most important question of their lives "Will you marry me?" Often my guests have no idea where to start or what to do. So I help them take it back to basics. What does your partner like, such as a special flower, song, fragrance or activity? What is it about them that you find special, and how can we incorporate that into your proposal? Do you want to pop the question in public or in private? What kind of budget are we working with? And most of all, how do we make the moment one that she'll never forget? I've arranged planes, helicopters and horse-drawn carriages. I have filled hotel suites so they are dripping with roses and hired a string quartet for the moment. I've arranged restaurant meals where the whole dining room is in on the event and ones where it is a total surprise to everyone. I have even arranged for the proposer to spray paint the question in a lane, graffiti style. Gratefully, I can say that we have all achieved a 100 % strike rate - everyone has said yes. It is truly a joy to be asked to assist with such special moments.

James Ridenour, Chef Concierge,
2nd Vice President, Les Clefs d'Or International

Personal Connections

As most of my colleagues who have served as a concierge for many years would agree, one of the greatest things about what we do is having the opportunity to meet a wide variety of people from different backgrounds. We get to see and interact with these individuals in a more personal way than most people. My personal story on this topic takes me back almost 20 years. A former regular guest of mine, whom I've known since she was in her late teens staying at my former hotel in New York, over the years became a very dear friend where I kindly asked her to be my younger son's godparent. Many years later, I flew halfway around the world to Barbados to take part in her very private wedding ceremony with her partner. For those of us who are genuinely interested in people, there's no better job in the world!

A. Burak Ipekci, Head Concierge
Hilton London Metropole

All They Needed Was a Sign

A hotel guest quietly approached my concierge desk. She had a handwritten note in her hand and slid it across the desk. The note revealed that she wanted to pamper her dog.

Being a dog lover, I was thrilled to be a part of this request! Now, he wasn't just any dog. He was her service dog, and she wanted him to have a special day. We arranged a special canine massage to start. Since the guest was hearing impaired, she communicated to the service dog in sign language. At the end of the day, the guest signed to her companion that she was grateful for his service. The service dog reacted in pure joy and affection towards his owner.

It was honestly the most beautiful interaction I've ever seen at a hotel concierge desk.

Laura Cunningham, Former Chef Concierge Nashville, Concierge in Philadelphia, Member Les Clefs d'Or

Stars in the Forest

After an in-depth hour-long conversation with a future guest about her upcoming trip to Baden-Baden and the Black Forest, I managed to put together a very full three-day itinerary per all her requests. As we were speaking about exploring the Black Forest, this curious future guest asked if it was possible to see the stars from "where we are." On the last evening of her stay, we ended up organizing a private viewing in the middle of the Black Forest Nature Reserve (where there is very little light pollution). After a short drive with our limousine service, our best guide took the family for an easy hike to a location where we had arranged for a halal barbeque and marshmallows over the fire. We also had an expert astrologer read the stars and tell stories about them.

This is a classic example of how we can create a "magical moment" out of a simple and genuine conversation. These unique, memorable moments define being a great concierge.

Sascha Domm, Chef Concierge
Brenners Park-Hotel & Spa, Baden-Baden

> "To laugh often and much; to win the respect of the intelligent people and the affection of children; to earn the appreciation of honest critics and endure the betrayal of false friends; to appreciate beauty; to find the beauty in others; to leave the world a bit better whether by a healthy child, a garden patch, or a redeemed social condition; to know that one life has breathed easier because you lived here. This is to have succeeded."

— RALPH WALDO EMERSON

Final Thoughts

One of the biggest takeaways I had from reading all of these stories is that *hospitality is universal*, going beyond cultural, language, and even physical boundaries. You can feel the enthusiasm, delight, and even pride through the moments shared.

I think it is fair to say that all of us have had the incredible pleasure and honor to be a part of a story in the lives of others. No task too small, no request too big, every interaction inspired by the genuine desire to make a difference in the lives of others.

This is hospitality from within.

About The Author

Sarah Dandashy is an internationally renowned hospitality consultant and travel expert. A former award-winning Les Clefs d'Or concierge, she has over 18 years of luxury hotel experience. Having built a 200+k global social media community of hoteliers and travelers, she continues to work with some of the leading brands in the travel industry as a content creator and spokesperson. Those brands include Marriott International, Hilton Hotels and Resorts, Four Seasons, Karisma Hotels and Resorts, Celebrity Cruises, Norwegian Cruise Line, and Allianz Travel Insurance. Sarah makes regular TV appearances on ABC, CBS, NBC, and FOX, and is a frequent guest on The Kelly Clarkson Show, Cheddar News, and Good Day LA. She has been featured in The New York Times, Business Insider, USNews, Reader's Digest, Nerdwallet, and Thrillist.